D0888700

GUIDE TO THE MONASTERY OF SAN LORENZO EL REAL

ALSO CALLED EL ESCORIAL

Juan Martínez Cuesta
Servicio de Conservación
Patrimonio Nacional

Photographs
Félix Lorrio

Translated by:
Richard-Lewis Rees

EDITORIAL PATRIMONIO NACIONAL
MADRID
1992

©EDITORIAL PATRIMONIO NACIONAL
All rights reserved
Palacio Real de Madrid
Calle de Bailén, s/n. - 28071 Madrid
ISBN: 84-7120-155-0
NIPO: 006-92-001-7
Depósito Legal: B-7726-1992
Printed by: LUNWERG EDITORES S.A.
Beethoven, 12 - 08021 Barcelona
Printed in Spain

CONTENTS

I. INTRODUCTION

About thirty miles (six and a half leagues) from Madrid, in the foothills of the Sierra de Guadarrama (3087 feet above sea level), the Monastery of of San Lorenzo el Real, known from its beginnings as El Escorial, has proudly stood, defying time and the inclemencies of the weather, for over four hundred years. The foundation of this colossal building was the brainchild of the equally prominent personage Philip II who, by carrying out this admirable project, sought to eternalise the glory of the Spanish monarchy embodied in the figures of his father, the Emperor Charles V, and he himself, as the perpetuator of the House of Austria.

Work began on the building on St. George's Day, April 23 1563, the foundation stone being laid in what was to the refectory, beneath the Prior's chair, accompanied by a simple ceremony presided over by Father Juan de Huete, the monastery's first Prior and member of the Order of St. Jerome. This occasion marked the end of a long period of preparation during which Philip II had gathered together all the elements necessary, both human and divine, to bring the enterprise to a successful conclusion, for from its very inception it had been conceived as something much more complex than the simple founding of a new religious establishment.

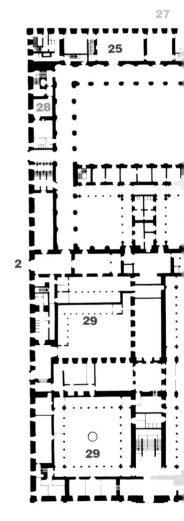

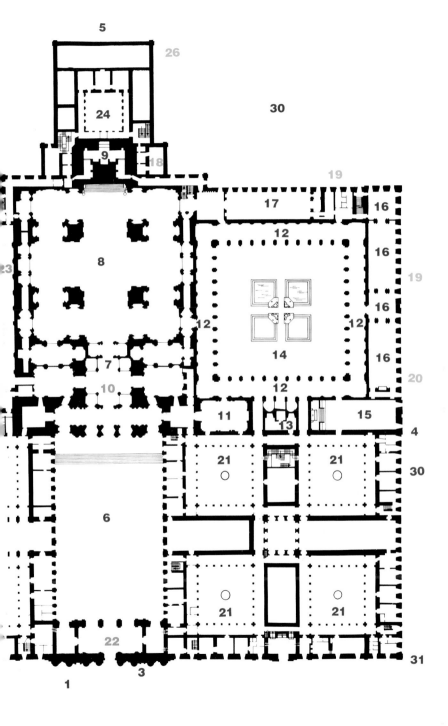

Motives for the Foundation

M any were the reasons which induced the king to take this decision, as we know from the *Carta de Fundación y Dotación* (Foundation Charter) issued in Madrid in 1567 when work was already under way. According to this document, the main motives were three:

- Firstly, to conceive a new monastery as an act of perpetual thanks for all the mercies granted by God.

- Secondly, to build and equip a temple in eternal memory of the Royal Family, with all due pomp and ceremony.

- Finally, to found a Royal Pantheon or House of Eternity in which the monarch's family be laid to rest, and that this be large enough for all the funeral rites to be carried out inside.

There were other, complementary, reasons for the foundation which have traditionally been considered fundamental. Among these is the excessive importance that has been attached to the Battle of San Quintín, which occurred in 1557. This military event is now seen for what it was, a further episode in the troubled relations between Spain and France in the XVI and XVII centuries, and in no way should it be classed as a reason for the origin of San Lorenzo.

Another argument to be considered is the strong bond of paternal and filial love established between Charles V and Philip II, although father and son were completely different in character. On the one hand, the Emperor, a man of action and an untiring traveller who went personally to solve problems wherever they occurred; on the other, Philip II, the first sedentary monarch in modern history, a meticulous, refined personality whose life was governed by moderation and prudence. Given this immense difference, it is easy to understand the son's great admiration for his father. When the latter died in the Monastery of Yuste, in 1558, he left the choice of his final resting place to his successor. In successive wills the Emperor had indicated two places where he wished to be buried: at first Innsbruck, next to his grandfather Maximillian, then the Carthusian monastery of Dijon, where the Duke and Duchess of the House of Burgundy lie. This change was due to the fact that the Emperor considered himself founder of the Spanish branch of the Habsburgs, which led him to think that Spain would be the ideal place to be buried. However, as there was no family pantheon for these new dynastic connotations, he left the choice of the place to Philip II.

The king, however, did not want to create a burial place for his father alone, but for the whole family. Philip II was a man who loved his family deeply, although this love was not always requited. When he took the decision to found a pantheon, this was to be not only for his parents and wives but also for the rest of the Royal Family and successor. In this way, the Monastery of San Lorenzo would become the dynastic confirmation of the House of Austria.

Construction of the Building

The exact reasons for the choice of this site have still to be clearly explained. Philip II appointed a commission, consisting of stonemasons, architects, astronomers, astrologers and theologians, who found this esplanade at the foot of the Sierra de Guadarrama to be the most salubrious. One of the most convincing theories justifies this choice as responding to the king's wish to build his monastery as close as possible to God, but without challenging his power; for this reason he situated it on the slope of the mountain and not on its summit, in order to avoid a second Tower of Babel. However, it was not this building from biblical times that the king had in mind, but the Temple of Jerusalem, built by Solomon. At a time of religious struggles caused by the Protestant reform, Philip II, the military arm of the Catholic Church, found in the execution of this project the affirmation of the power of the Gospel over any attempted schism.

For the construction of this building, Philip II turned to a number of different professional artists and craftsmen. In 1559 he called back from Naples the Spanish architect Juan Bautista de Toledo, who had been working on the Basilica of St. Peter's as Michaelangelo's main assistant. His journey, however, was marked by tragedy, as his family perished and his library was lost. These terrible misfortunes and the many responsibilities he was given transformed him into a sickly man with depressive tendencies. In 1561 the military engineer Francesco Paciotto was called, who severely criticised Toledo's project and drew up the plans for the church, which the king accepted. These plans follow Galeazzo Alessi's ideas for Santa Maria de Carignano, and not Michaelangelo's model for the Vatican Basilica. Finally, mention must be made of the figure of Juan de Herrera, appointed assistant to Juan Bautista de Toledo by Philip II. His role in the construction of the monastery was fundamental since, after Toledo's death in 1567, he took charge of the latter's works and projects, managing to complete them in the shortest possible time.

Work on the Monastery of San Lorenzo began on April 23

The snow-bound Monastery from the Huerta de los Frailes.

1563, with the laying of the first stone on the southern façade. That same year the foundations were laid for the palace and for the far end of the church, and the southern and western sides were begun. The following year it was decided that the building should be extended, since the monastery part was considered to be too small. The solution consisted in raising it to the same height as the palace and joining the roofs in a uniform whole, thus endowing the building with its characteristic appearance. Work proceeded at a furious pace, since in 1565 the foundations were laid for the rest of the building and in 1571 the Hieronymite community occupied the southwestern wing, which had by then been completed.

That year the mortal remains of the Imperial Family began to arrive and were laid provisionally beneath the altar of the Church of El Prestado, the chapel in which mass was held until the basilica was finished; in this way the series of religious and funeral rites the king had planned was set in motion. In 1574 work began on the basilica, to be completed on June

Night-time view of San Lorenzo from "La Horizontal".

23 1582 with the placing of the dome. At the same time work began on the library and the royal dependencies around the Patio de los Mascarones, situated at the back end of the basilica.

Although the building's last stone was placed, on the top left-hand side of the Patio de los Reyes, on September 13 1584, the decoration programmes had still to be fully carried out. They were finally completed in 1600, two years after the death of Philip II, with the placing of his statue, in an attitude of prayer, and those of his family on the basilica's main altar. The only project left incomplete was the pantheon as we know it today, built during the reigns of Philip III and Philip IV and finished in 1654.

The Layout

The whole architectural mass of the building, both in ground plan and elevation, can be reduced to two geometrical figures: the square and the rectangle. A close examination of the plan of the monastery reveals how the whole complex is in the form of a square divided lengthwise into three rectangles. In the central one the Patio de los Reyes, the church and the private palace are situated; to the left stand the school and the public palace, and to the right the monastery. These same cubic forms are also repeated in the patios, where we see that the square predominates opposite the Patio de los Reyes and the Patio de los Coches, which follow the proportions of the Golden Rectangle as a sign of the importance of these patios over the remainder. This is the singular layout that XIX-century travellers compared to a *parrilla* or grille, the symbol of the martyrdom of St. Lawrence, although strangely enough this never occurred to the monastery's creators.

The alternation between these two geometrical forms is repeated throughout the complex until a "whole" is formed that could be defined as rigid, symmetrical and balanced. San Lorenzo first strikes the visitor as a world closed in upon itself, a self-sufficient environment from which Philip II could govern, pray and honour his ancestors. For these very reasons the building was arranged perfectly to fulfil the function for which it was conceived: to be the spiritual and renovating centre of the new Europe born from the Council of Trent. We must not forget that the construction of the monastery was the expression in stone of the king's intellectual concept of the world, to the extent that even today, four hundred years later, the idea, though no longer applicable, still lives on.

The Chroniclers of San Lorenzo

T he construction of this building aroused the interest of contemporaries from the very day of its foundation. This interest has since then been on the increase, evidence of which is the preparation of this guidebook which, together with previous publications and those to come, sets out to show the visitor the grandeur of the Monastery of San Lorenzo.

Those originally most interested in the building were its first occupants, the Hieronymite brothers, and it is thanks to different monks from the order that we have the first news of its construction and its description once completed. The most prominent among these was Fray Antonio de Villacastín, the master builder involved in the work and a lay brother from the Monastery of La Sisla, Toledo. Villacastín came to San Lorenzo early in June 1562, where he resided until his death in 1603. His work, published under the title of *Memorias*, is a book of notes on the construction. We continue with the figure of Fray Juan de San Jerónimo, a founder brother who also lived in the monastery until his death, which occurred in 1591. His writings on the building follow the same pattern as those of Villacastín. Finally, within this particular block mention must be made of Fray Jerónimo de Sepúlveda whose work, published under the title of *Historia de varios sucesos y de las cosas notables que han acaecido en España y en otras naciones desde el año 1584 hasta el de 1603* (History of events and notable occurrences that have taken place in Spain and other nations between 1584 and 1603), includes the first description of the completed monastery.

The most important of the historians of San Lorenzo, however, is Fray José de Sigüenza whose work, *La Fundación del Monasterio de El Escorial,* published in 1605, is essential to an understanding of the building. This volume forms part of a much larger work which, under the title of *Historia de la Orden de San Jerónimo,* set out to extol the virtues and greatness of this religious order. The part concerning us here forms books III and IV of the study, where the author gives a detailed history of the foundation and construction of the monastery and

a description of all its parts. His style is clear, precise and realistic, and he presents events with objectivity.

The only outstanding XVII-century work is the book by Fray Francisco de los Santos which, titled *Descripción del Real Monasterio de San Lorenzo de El Escorial, única maravilla del mundo*, which is in fact a paraphrase of Sigüenza's description. The book is divided into two parts, the first of which is purely descriptive while the second is devoted to the completion of the Royal Pantheon and the transfer of the royal remains to their new resting place. This text was reprinted four times during the XVII century, which allowed the author to correct and add to the information it contains. In its final edition, published in Madrid in 1698, there is a description of the reconstruction work carried out during the reign of Charles II after it was razed to the ground by fire in 1671, and of Lucas Jordán's decorative work for the church and the main staircase.

During the XVIII century two descriptions of the building appeared which, though close to each other in time, are completely different in character. The first is the work of Fray Andrés Ximénez, published in Madrid in 1764 under the title of *Descripción del Real Monasterio de San Lorenzo del Escorial, su magnífico Templo, Panteón y Palacio....* His writings follow the tradition established by Sigüenza. The second writer is Antonio Ponz, whose book constitutes the second volume of his ambitious work *Viaje de España* (Journey through Spain) published between 1772 and 1794. Although his text merely describes the building, his spirit is that of a man of the Enlightenment. He takes data from previous authors and uses them for purely informative purposes, in keeping with the intellectual spirit of the reign of Charles III.

The XIX century was to have a profound effect on the life of San Lorenzo. On the one hand the Napoleonic invasion, and on the other the confiscation and sale of church lands, known as *desamortización,* transformed the monastery into a controversial symbol of the old regime and of Spanish imperialist politics. Outstanding among the authors who write about the building are Fray Damián Bermejo and Fray José Quevedo, the last of the Hieronymite brothers to leave us a description of their residence, conscious as they were of its historical relevance. Finally, mention must be made of the work of Antonio de Rotondo, published in Madrid in 1863, the first illustrated description of the monastery.

With the XX century came a new kind of description which we call the "guidebook", and we include in this literary genre all the most recent publications, including this one, whose purpose is to show the visitor the greatness of a monument which in 1984 was declared by UNESCO to be part of the World Heritage.

II. DESCRIPTION AND HISTORY

Main façade from The Lonja.

1. FAÇADES

The Lonja

E ntry to the monastery is through the *Lonja*, a large granite-paved area that runs around the northern and western sides of the building. The precinct is enclosed by a low wall or *períbolo* which limits the holy site, or *témenos*, upon which the monastery stands. The village of San Lorenzo de El Escorial has respected the contours of the monastery, since it extends only on the northern and western sides of the building, thus limiting contact between it and the outside world to these two façades only.

The Northern and Western Façades

T he northern façade is the most impressive of all, by virtue of its austere decoration in which the building's first enigma is supposed to be found, the key to which has yet to be discovered. The situation of doors and windows creates a rhythm which, in combination with the horizontal divisions, on the basis of **smooth beading,** and the great vertical cornice, an element that runs all around the building, defines the force and hermeticism of its creators. The entrances to the royal residence are situated here, both the main one (the first door), and the one for the servants, which is now the visitors' access. The third door is the service entrance for the college. This façade was thoroughly remodelled by Juan de Villanueva in 1793 when it had to be adapted to the needs of the Bourbon court, as we shall see when we examine the Palace of Charles IV.

The main façade is on the western side, looking towards Monte Abantos and with its back to Madrid. This situation is surprising, since the part of a building we normally see first is its main façade, which in this case is hidden from the observer. This layout forms part of the itinerary established for

The college tower.

entry into the building. After leaving the northern side, because of its orientation the most lugubrious, we come to the main façade, bathed in light and the symbol of Jesus Christ. On this side we find the main entrances to the school, the monastery and, in the middle, the church. All the entrances are elegantly finished, the most outstanding element being the complex corresponding to the main door, which rises two floors above the roof line and houses the library. The main entrance is conceived as two sections encompassing a total of six storeys and a seventh which contains the lofts. The first section is flanked by eight gigantic Tuscan columns, four on either side of the door, between which niches and blind windows have been inserted, creating effects of light and shade. Above the door lintel, on both sides of the window, appear two grids, the symbol of the martyrdom of St. Lawrence. The second section is composed of four gigantic Ionic columns, in the central space between which we see the coat of arms of the founder, Philip II, and a statue of the deacon Lawrence,

*Main façade with the coat of arms of the Founder and
the statue of St. Lawrence.*

the saint to whom the building is dedicated. Outstanding in
the sculptural composition on this façade, the work of the
Toledan artist Juan Bautista Monegro, is the sculpture of the
saint from Huesca. This singular piece is in granite and is
over four metres tall. The head, feet and hands were realised
in white marble and the grid he holds in his right hand is of
gilt bronze. The saint appears as a young man, symbolising
vigour and selfless service to the Church, is dressed in an elegant dalmatic and holds a book in his left hand.

The composition is crowned with a large pediment with
granite balls acting as acroteria.

The Southern and Eastern Façades

The southern façade is the most balanced of all, the horizontality of the windows and the lack of vertical divisions conferring upon it its impressive appearance. It is here that Juan de Herrera's contribution to the construction of the monastery can best be appreciated, since its present-day appearance has nothing to do with the one conceived by Juan Bautista Toledo. In Toledo's project this façade, as well as the northern one, had a tower in the middle (traces of which can still be seen) and a difference in heights marked by this tower. On eliminating this element, the surface is conceived on the basis of the Golden Rectangle, achieving the perfection and harmony that characterise the façade.

We finish with the eastern façade, of the four the richest in terms of volumes. In the middle there is an added wing containing the royal rooms and above, the austere church frontispiece. On either side stand the monastery and the public palace, each one terminating in a tower, known as the Torre del Prior and the Torre de Damas.

Patio de Reyes, temple façade.

2. THE PATIO DE REYES

After passing through the large entrance hall we come to the Patio de Reyes (Kings' Patio), whose name derives from the sculptures contained there. This patio, of perfect proportions (64 x 38 m), was conceived as the anteroom to the basilica and as a point of union between divine and human wisdom. Its four sides correspond to the library, with direct access; the college and the monastery as the two options of life in the faith: militant and contemplative; and the large façade of the church which is presented as the new Temple of Solomon. This idea, to which reference was made earlier, here seems to attain its true significance.

Let us now pause before the church façade. It is divided into five sections by Doric columns with gigantic order bases, which frame the semicircular arches and the balconies above. The three central arches, which jut out, serve as the entrance to the basilica, while the one on the right provides access to the monastery and the one on the left to the palace. The balconies, which are now closed, were originally the points from which mass was held, since on the central one stands the altar which featured Benvenuto Cellini's *Christ* before it was moved to the basilica. These architectural elements are the foremost precedent to the open chapels built in the religious foundations of the New World. In the second section of the façade we find sculptures of the six kings of Judah who participated in the construction of the Biblical temple. In the middle appears David, with the harp and the sword as symbols of the musician and warrior king; and Solomon, book in hand, the prototype of the wise king. It is to these two monarchs that we owe the construction of the temple, as the Latin inscriptions on the bases tell us. To our right we find Josiah, with a roll of parchment symbolising one volume of the Book of Deuteronomy which he found when he reconstructed the temple; and Manasseh, with a compass and a square, instruments he used in the restoration of the temple and the walls of Jerusalem in repentance for having worshipped the pagan gods. To our left we have Hezekia, holding a navicula in his left hand and a billy goat between his legs, which symbolise the restoration of the sacrificial altar he ordered to be built during his reign. Finally we have Josaphat with an axe in his left hand, since he commanded that the woods in which the people worshipped the false gods be cut down, and a lamb and loaves of bread at his feet, since he reintroduced the practice of sacrifices in the temple. All the sculptures were produced by Monegro in granite, with the heads, hands and feet in white marble. The kings are all wear crowns and carry sceptres, symbols executed in gilt bronze. These additional elements, together with some of the previously mentioned ones, are by Sebastián Fernández.

The façade is crowned by a Syrian style pediment, in the centre of which we see the great window which illuminates the basilica choir. The composition is framed by the two belfries which, together with the dome, are the highest points of the monastery.

In 1988 the carillon donated by the Community of Madrid

View of the library façade from the statue of King Hezekia.

was installed in the left-hand tower. Following the Flemish custom, Philip II endowed the monastery with a "bell organ" or carillon, built by Peter van der Ghein. This instrument was destroyed in the great fire of 1671, so Charles II commissioned Melchor de Haze to build a second carillon. The present-day instrument was made by the Dutch master craftsman André Lehr and it can be considered a reconstruction of the one built late in the XVII century, since the bells remaining from this one were used for the new instrument. Each bell bears the coat of arms of the monastery and of Her Majesty Queen Sofía, to whom the instrument is dedicated.

3. THE CHURCH

T he axis around which the building revolves is the church, also known as the basilica, since this was the name given to the palaces that the Emperor Constantine converted into Christian churches. When Father Ximénez calls this area the "basilica", he does so not only because he considers it a royal house, but also because of the altars it contains dedicated to the cult of relics.

The church is divided into four parts, a structure that reflects that of Spanish society in the XVI century. The common people are situated in the atrium, the aristocracy in the temple, the religious community in the choir and the monarchs in their oratories in the presbytery.

Having passed through the *Patio de Reyes* we come to a covered area or large vaulted hall corresponding to the narthex of ancient Roman basilicas. This porticoed gallery has the same openings as the façade. The three central ones provide entry into the basilica, and above them we find the black marble medallions alluding to the placing of the first stone on St. Bernard's Day, August 20 1563, and its consecration on August 30 1595. The doors were of *ácana* wood, a West Indian construction timber, and the panels in ilex.

The Atrium

T he first of the church's sections is known today as the *sotocoro* or atrium, although originally it was called the "body of the church" by virtue of its function. According to Father Sigüenza, this section was used as the church for the people and for the king's servants in order to prevent the lower social groups occupying the same place as the aristocracy. Its structure, in the form of a Greek cross inserted into a square and crowned by a dome, follows the same layout as the basilica and constitutes a temple on a genuinely human scale. The most important element is its "flat" vault, consisting of eight concentric stone rings which serve to deflect all the weight of

the choir, situated above, to the four pillars upon which it rests. On the sides we find two doors which communicate with the *patinejo* of the palace, on our left, and the *patinejo* (small courtyard of the monastery, on our right.

The decoration of the atrium is limited to two altars where we find the model of paired saints that figures on the canvases that decorate all the chapels. On our right, *San Cosme and San Damián*, the doctor martyrs, much worshipped by the populace, and on our right, *St. Sixtus, Pope, and St. Blas, Bishop,* as models of ecclesiastical authority; both paintings were begun by Juan Fernández Navarrete "el Mudo" (the Mute) and finished by Diego de Urbina.

Before entering the temple we pass through the "choir of the seminaries", the place reserved for the seminarists who sang the dawn mass every day. This area contains only the long walnut bench on which they sat.

The Temple

After passing by the bronze grille, wrought and gilt in the Tujarón workshops in Zaragoza, we enter the temple. Its ground plan is in the form of a Greek cross inserted in a square in whose centre, resting on four enormous pilasters, we find the dome, 276 feet above the floor. opposite the pilasters are eight pillars on the side walls which support twenty-four semicircular arches, distributing the weight of the dome and the eight vaults in the strictest possible classical style. The Tuscan order pillars are decorated by fluted shafts.

The central pillars, on the sides that look onto the lateral aisles, and the wall pillars, are divided vertically into two sections and are crowned by semicircular arches; the lower sections are for the chapels while the upper ones house the gallery with gilt bronze parapets. A passageway runs around the whole temple area thirty feet off the ground, the same height as the galleries. The whole complex is lit by ten windows thermal and the ten in the dome. The vaults are of brick and were originally stuccoed in white, almost certainly with blue stars, until by order of Charles II Lucas Jordán redecorated them between 1692 and 1694. The flooring is entirely of white and grey marble from Granada and Alemtejo (Portugal).

Iconographical programme

Distributed among the forty-five altars in the temple we find one of the few iconographical programmes of Spanish religious art that have been preserved *in situ*. The decoration consists entirely of paintings and was commissioned from Spanish artists, except the reliquaries, which were painted by Federico Zuccaro, although Philip II subsequently ordered Juan Goméz to retouch them. Each altar consists of an altar stone in granite and grey marble. The canvases are in simple gilt frames, above which are circular plaster pediments made by José Marzal in 1829. The decoration was commissioned from the court painter, Juan Fernández Navarrete, called "the Mute", who began this task in 1576. On his death in 1579, it was decided that the programme should be completed by Diego de Urbina, Alonso Sánchez Coello and Luis de Carvajal. We begin our itinerary at the first section, from the presbytery, where we find eight chapels together with the two reliquary altars on both sides of the main altar. In each painting we find a pair of full-length portraits of saints and the attributes that distinguish them. The subjects chosen are the Twelve Apostles and the Four Evangelists who, together with the Virgin Mary and St. Jerome (in the reliquaries), constitute the pillars of the Church. The saints are arranged in the following way:

1. On the left-hand side:
- St. Peter and St. Paul
- St. Philip and St. James the Younger
- St. John the Evangelist and St. Matthew
- St. Mark and St. Luke

2. On the right-hand side:
- St. Bartholemew and St. Thomas
- St. Barnaby and St. Matthias
- St. James the Elder and St. Andrew
- St. Simon and St. Judas.

All the paintings are by Navarrete "el Mudo".

3. The Reliquaries. Following another of the precepts approved by the Council of Trent, referring to the worship of saints, Philip II endowed the monastery with one of the richest collections of relics from the Catholic Church which, according to Father Sigüenza, "we know of no saint of whom there are no relics here except St. Joseph, St. John the Evangelist and St. James the Elder, the latter preserved in his entirety in his own church in Compostela". During the time of the founder over seven thousand relics were collected together and kept in five hundred boxes or reliquaries, most of which were built by the silversmith Juan de Arfe in a wide variety of forms: heads, if they were for skulls, arms, if they were for limb bones, pyramids and chests, among others. The relics were distributed throughout the monastery, the most important of them being concentrated in the basilica on the two altars built for the purpose. On the left-hand side, beneath the protection of the Mystery of the Annunciation, all the bones of feminine saints and martyrs were kept. On the opposite side, on the altar of St. Jerome, all the remains of male saints and martyrs were placed. These large cupboards are divided into two sections, which can be opened at the front so that the relics can be worshipped, and at the rear in order to gain access to them.

"Reliquary of the Annunciation",
by Zúccaro.

The task of decorating them was entrusted to Federico Zuccaro who, on the left-hand side, depicted the *Annunciation of the Virgin Mary*. At the top we find *St. Maurice, St. Louis, King of France, St. Malcolm, King, St. Margaret, Queen, St. Isabella, Queen of Portugal,* and *St. Gereón,* the work of Bartolomé Carducho.

On the right-hand side appears *St. Jerome in the Desert,* the work of Zuccaro retouched by Juan Gómez. At the top we have *St. Constance, martyr, St. Charlemagne, St. Arnulf, St. Bega, St. William* and *St. Mercury, martyr,* by Martín Gómez.

Next, and following the itinerary to the altar, we find the following chapels:

First Chapel

Dedicated to the precursors of Christ. Here we find *St. Anne,* whose face is said to be that of Anne of Austria, the last wife of Philip II, and *St. John the Baptist preaching,* both canvases are by Luca Cambiasso.

Second Chapel

Next to the central canvas depicting *St. Michael,* the work of Tibaldi, we have four doctors of the Spanish Church, *St. Ildefonso and St. Eugene of Toledo* and *St. Isidore and St. Leander,* both by Luis de Carvajal.

Third Chapel

The altar is presided over by *The Martyrdom of St. Maurice and the Theban Legion,* by Rómulo Cincinato, the canvas that replaced the one by El Greco now in the *Salón de Honor.* At the end of the nave there is a group of martyrs, *St. Fabian and St. Sebastian* by Diego de Urbina, *St. Justo and St. Pastor* and *St. Lawrence and St. Stephen* by Sánchez Coello.

Fourth Chapel

Also known as the Chapel of the Church Fathers or of the Doctors. The four fathers of the Latin Church appear: *St. Ambrose and St. Gregory* by Urbina, and *St. Jerome and St. Augustin* by Sánchez Coello. Next to these are the four fathers of the Eastern Church: *St. Gregory Naciancene and St. John Chrisostome* by Carvajal and *St. Basil and St. Atanasio* by Sánchez Coello. The set is completed by *St. Buenaventura and St. Thomas* by Carvajal. The presence of the Holy Doctors is justified by the fact that it was through this chapel that the teachers and students entered and left the basilica. Next to the door we see the two-spouted font where people could wash. This chapel was also the entrance for the king's knights through the palace patio. During the reign of Charles III this access was closed and now standing there is the altar with Cellini's magnificent *Christ*.

This sculpture was made by Benvenuto Cellini between 1559 and 1562 to preside over his own grave, which was to be situated in the Church of the Nunziata in Florence. According to the sculptor himself, he felt obliged to present it as a gift to the Duke and Duchess of Toscana, since they praised it so highly one day when they visited his studio. The work remained in the Pitti Palace until 1576, when it set sail for Spain thanks to the generosity of the Duke and Duchess, who in their turn presented it as a gift to Philip II. On November 9 that same year it reached the Palace of El Pardo, from whence it was carried on the backs of fifty bearers to the monastery. Its final position was in the choir just behind the Prior's Chair, where it remained until 1965, when a new location was sought where visitors could contemplate it without disturbing the peace of the place of worship. Cellini conceived his Christ on the Cross as an Apolline figure, whose body of dazzling beauty breathes harmony and serenity. The figure of Christ bears no signs of the torment to which he was subjected, the essence of his grandeur lying in his balance of passions. The artist chose to do without any accessory element so that our attention is focused on the meaning of the sacrifice on the Cross as the triumph over death. The work was made from a great block of white Carrara marble. At first it was thought that the sculpture was of a single piece, but a closer examination reveals that the arms were added subsequently, although with such mastery that when the Napoleonic troops removed them, it was said that they had had to use saws.

To our left we see a modern image of the Virgin of Consolation, venerated by the Order of St. Augustin.

We leave this chapel to find on the left-hand side the altar of *St. Paul the Hermit and St. Anthony the Abbot* by Sánchez Coello, which forms a pair with the altar of the right-hand side representing *St. Martha and St. Mary Magdalene* by Diego de Urbina. Both constitute exaltation of the monastic life.

We now move over to the right-hand side, which contains the same number of chapels and altars as the other. Our itinerary now follows the chapels numerically from the last to the first.

Fourth Chapel or Chapel of the Holy Virgins and Martyrs

Here we find two groups; on the one side that of the martyrs: *St. Leocadia and St. Engracia,* and *St. Cecily and St. Barbara,* both by Carvajal, *St. Agueda and St. Lucia* by Urbina, and *St. Catherine and St. Agnes* by Sánchez Coello; on the other that of the holy founders: *St. Clare and St. Escolástica* (Franciscans of the Order of St. Clare and Benedictines) and *St. Paula and St. Monica* (Hieronymites and Augustinians) by Urbina. This chapel is an apology of Virginity, a virtue which the Catholic Church, after the Council of Trent, considered to be one of the most important values of contemplative religious life. Today it contains the Holy Sacrament, so that the visitor can wander freely through the rest of the temple without disturbing the peace of those who enter to pray. As with the Chapel of the Doctors, here was the entrance from the monastery side, today closed and occupied by the altar of the Virgin of Patronage, Patron Saint of the Monastery of San Lorenzo, whose statue was donated by Philip IV. At the back end we see a sculpture representing *Christ Crucified* dedicated to *la Buena Muerte* (Good Death), a XVII-century Spanish work.

We now return to the nave, where there is a further group of holy martyrs, namely *St. Martin and St. Nicholas*, *St. Anthony of Padua and St. Peter the Martyr,* both by Carvajal, and *St. Vincent and St. George* by Sánchez Coello.

Third Chapel

This area is not decorated, since it serves as a link with the lower main cloister, and is referred to as the *Puerta de las Procesiones* (Processions Gate), since it was through here that the solemn processions held inside the monastery entered and left. This custom still persists today among the Augustinian Community.

Second Chapel

This chapel is dedicated to the founding fathers of western religious orders: *St. Dominic and St. Francis of Assisi* (Dominicans and Franciscans) by Carvajal and *St. Benedict and St. Bernard* (Benedictines and Cistercians) by Sánchez Coello. In the middle, coinciding with the central axis of the basilica, *The Martyrdom of St. Ursula and the Eleven Thousand Virgins* by Tibaldi. Together with its companion, *St. Michael,* on the opposite side, this canvas was originally commissioned from Luca Cambiasso, who did actually paint them. However, they were not to Philip II's liking and were consequently replaced by Tibaldi's works.

First Chapel

This chapel was never decorated with paintings and serves as access to the sacristy and the pantheons. The altar of the Virgin of Patronage, now worshipped in the Chapel of the Virgins, originally stood here.

The description of the decoration of the temple is completed with Lucas Jordán's frescoes. These are on the vaults, only the dome being left unadorned. The iconographical programme, devised by Charles II and the Prior, Father Alonso de Talavera, is an exaltation of the Virgin Mary and the Eucharist, dogmas of faith for which members of the House of Austria had shown particular devotion since the time of Philip II.

On the Altar of the Annunciation we find the theme of *The Word Made Flesh* with representations of *The Annunciation*, *The Birth of Christ* and *The Adoration of the Kings*. On the opposite side, on the Altar of St. Jerome we see the saint himself before Christ and the Celestial Court, accused of having made a profound study of the writings of pagan antiquity. In the centre, on the vault before the presbytery, appears *The Death, Burial and Ascent of the Virgin Mary*.

On the opposite vault on the left-hand side can be seen the *Ecclesia Militans* or triumph of the Militant Church, accompanied by the Virtues, the Liberal Arts and the Church Fathers. On the opposite side, *The Glorification of the Immaculate Conception* features the Virgin enthroned in a triumphal carriage accompanied by angels, holy virgins, women martyrs, holy widows and women from the Old Testament. In the middle, as the final episode in the History of Salvation, *The Last Judgment*.

The programme was completed with the passages on the second floor of the basilica, where scenes from the life of Solomon appear on the northern side, together with the Triumph of the Church, since it is here that access is gained to the school and, just beneath, the Chapel of the Doctors is located. On the northern side, where the entrance to the choir from the monastery stands, we see scenes from the life of David, the king who composed the psalms that the monks sang in praise of The Lord.

The only frescoes that do not follow this subject matter are the ones on the cross nave of the basilica. After arduous discussions between the king, the prior and the painter himself, Lucas Jordán, it was decided to decorate it with scenes from the Old Testament. On the northern side we see *The Passage through the Red Sea*, *The Builders of the Ark of the Covenant*, *Bezahleel and Oholiab*, *Manna Falling from Heaven* and *Samson and the Lion in whose Jaws he Found a Honeycomb*. On the southern side we see *Joshua's Victory over the Amalekites*, *Gideon, Othniel, Yefté and Abdón*, *Elías is Given Bread by the Angel* and *David Receives the Holy Loaves from the High Priest*.

In the middle of the temple, in the transept naves, the great

Lucas Jordán: "The Resurrection and The Last Judgment".

candelabra are kept which were made in gilt bronze by the Flemish craftsman Juan Simón in 1571. Their respective names are The Carnation and The Tenebrae Hearse and they were used for the Offices of Holy Week.

The Presbytery

We now come to the culminating point of the basilica: the presbytery, the place where Holy Mass is heard. The main chapel is conceived as a large space forming the head of the main nave of the temple. This chapel is totally differentiated from the rest of the religious building by virtue of the richness of its materials: Spanish marble and jasper of different colours. Its use was restricted to the priests who performed the sacrifice of the Eucharist. Twelve steps lead up to it, and then a further seven upon which the sacrificial stone sits. This latter flight serves to raise the whole complex to be perfectly visible from any point in the basilica, especially from the choir.

Our description begins with the altarpiece, designed by Juan de Herrera although it was built entirely by foreign artists and craftsmen. It is made from coloured marble and jasper, gilt bronze, and features oil paintings on canvas. This mixture of materials is indicative of the complexity and technical difficulties involved, since in Spain there were no artists who worked with these materials. I refer to the realisation of sculptures in gilt bronze, a highly costly task requiring specially skilled workmanship. They were made in Italy although the final gilting process was carried out in Madrid where Pompeius Leoni, the sculptor, set up a workshop specially for this purpose. In the Spanish tradition polychrome wood predominates over painting, but this is not the case in San Lorenzo.

The altarpiece begins with a raised socle upon which the first body rests, consisting of six freestanding columns, thus creating a *pentapartite* rhythm in which two "streets" appear reserved for the sculptures, two for painting and, in the cen-

Main Altar Reredos.

Tabernacle. The work of Jacoppo da Trezzo.

tral one, the tabernacle. This same layout is repeated in the second body in which the central "street" is replaced by a canvas. The order is broken in the third body and the attic, due to the great projection of the presbytery, forcing the classical proportions to be altered, creating much more slender and totally mannerist forms.

The order of the subjects obeys the rigid principles laid down by the Council of Trent with a view to exalting the Catholic dogma which had been rejected by the Protestant reform. The first body symbolises the presence of Christ on Earth, the latter represented by two adorations: *The Adoration of the Shepherds* and *The Adoration of the Wise Men*, both by Tibaldi. In the centre is the most important manifestation: the Eucharist, to house which the tabernacle was created.

It is customary in all tabernacles to find a shrine in which to keep the Holy Forms. According to how the altarpiece develops, this element may acquire greater importance and reaches its culmination in this temple, where it is presented as a freestanding form. This piece, a unique gem in its genre, was designed by Herrera and built by the Italian silversmith Jacoppo da Trezzo, who began work in 1579 and did not complete it until seven years later. The tabernacle, of different coloured marble and jasper, is conceived as a small circular temple crowned by a dome and framed with gilt bronze. The whole group rests on a rich jasper socle from which rise eight columns in this same material. The sculptures are located between the columns of the temple, where the four evangelists appear; on the cornice stand eight apostles and on top of the dome the figure of the Saviour. The whole work is in gilt bronze. The doors of the tabernacle correspond to the four cardinal points and inside, contained in a casket of pure gold and precious stones, beneath a topaz the size of a fist, the Eucharist was originally displayed. All this, however, disappeared during the Napoleonic invasion.

Behind the tabernacle we find a room or small chamber entered by means of the two mahogany doors lined with coloured jasper, situated on both sides of the altar on the socle. In order to illuminate this piece a window was placed in the wall, thus creating the first "transparent" in Spanish art. The interior of this piece, the true dwelling place of God, is covered in red and white marble and decorated with fresco paintings by Pellegrino Tibaldi. The subjects chosen are prefigurations of the Eucharist, related in the Old Testament: *Abraham Offers Melquisedec the Tithe of Victory*, *The Israelites Gathering Manna*, *The Legal Supper of Lamb*, and *Elías Fed by the Angel*. Finally, covering the great arch that serves as the ceiling, Tibaldi painted the Rainbow.

This body is completed with statues of the Four Doctors of the Western Church: St. Augustin, St. Jerome, St. Gregory and St. Ambrose.

The second body symbolises the Passion of Christ and the cult of the Saints. In the middle appears *The Martyrdom of St. Lawrence* by Tibaldi, and on either side *The Flagellation* and *Jesus Bearing the Cross*, both by Zuccaro. Framing the group are statues of the four Evangelists accompanied by their respective symbols.

The third floor is conceived as a body of glory. On either side *The Resurrection* and the *Pentecost* and in the middle *The Ascent of the Virgin Mary*, all by Federico Zuccaro. The group is completed with the sculptures of two apostles: *St. James*, Patron Saint of Spain, and *St. Andrew*, Patron Saint of the Order of the Golden Fleece.

The composition is closed in the attic with the sculpture of Christ on the Cross between the Virgin Mary and St. John, the subject known by the name of the *Calvary*. The wood used for the cross is the same as that from which Philip II's coffin was made, and came from the keel of the Spanish ship "Cinco Llagas" (Five Wounds). On either side we see *St. Peter* and *St. Paul*, pillars of the Roman Church. The sculpture of *St. Paul* is signed and dated on the base: *Pompeius Leoni fecit 1588*. The altarpiece was finally completed on September 6 1590 with the placing of the *Calvary*.

On either side of the main altar stand the oratories and royal cenotaphs. With these two elements the rigid iconographical programme was completed of the representation of the King within the order of etiquette imposed by Philip II on

*Philip II and his family
at prayer.*

the Spanish Court. The new system established that the power of the King came directly from God and he was responsible for his actions only to Him. This concept impregnated all the activities in the life of the monarch, transforming him into a divine being whose presence was comparable to that of God and, therefore, worthy of veneration. The figure of the King received special treatment at Court, with the ultimate objective of his presence never being seen but always felt. This explains the layout of the sides of the main altar, with two oratories, one for the King and the other for the Queen, hidden from the gaze of the Court, and two statue groups in which the Imperial and Royal Families appear in a permanent attitude of prayer, symbolising the eternal real presence of the sovereigns before the Supreme Maker. The oratories form part of the temple and lead directly into the royal chambers. Their doors are five steps below the entrance doors to the shrine or house of God. The dwelling of the monarchs, as beings chosen by God, frames the holy dwelling and their presence, temporal in the oratories and eternal in the cenotaphs, remains imperturbable before the Highest. On the left-hand side, beneath a great bearing arch and made of coloured marble and jasper with additions in gilt bronze, there are three doors, the first opening into the rear end of the Reliquary of the Annunciation and the remaining two into the queen's oratory. Above, and occupying the whole span of the arch, in the form of a wide gallery divided into three sections by two Tuscan columns, appears the sculptural group of the Imperial Family. Presiding over the group is Charles V, in armour and a flowing cloak featuring the two-headed eagle. To his right is his wife, Isabella of Portugal, and behind Mary of Austria, the Emperor's daughter, Mary of Hungary and Eleanor of France, both sisters of Charles V. Behind the group were placed five inscriptions in Latin alluding to the dignity of the figures represented and stating that the rest of the tribune, which is empty, can be occupied only by those descendants whose acts surpass those of the Emperor. Crowning this body is the imperial coat of arms, surrounded by the collar of the Golden Fleece and with the imperial crown above.

On the opposite side, and in accordance with this same structure, we find a further three doors, the first of which is the entrance for the priests who say Mass while the remaining two open into the king's oratory. Above is the group depicting the Royal Family at prayer, headed by Philip II dressed in armour and a cloak and accompanied by Anne of Austria, his fourth wife and mother of the heir. Behind we see Isabelle of Valois, his third wife, Prince Charles and his mother, Mary of Portugal, the king's first wife. Decorating the walls we see another group of Latin inscriptions referring to the dignity of the figures present and to the fact that the remaining spaces are reserved for those monarchs who surpass Philip II in virtue. Above is the King's coat of arms, enveloped in the Golden Fleece and bearing the crowns of the whole Iberian Peninsula, Sicily and Jerusalem.

The decoration of the presbytery is completed with the vault paintings, the work of Luca Cambiasso. The chosen motif is *The Coronation of the Virgin*, surrounded by the four major prophets with their respective symbols. The subject is related to the one appearing on the altarpiece and can be considered the colophon of this iconographical programme.

The pulpits and the lamp at the foot of the main altar were made during the reign of Ferdinand VII. The two marble and gilt bronze pulpits are the work of Manuel de Urquiza, bronzesmith to His Majesty. The one on the left-hand side depicts the four Evangelists with the royal coat of arms and is crowned by a figurine symbolising Religion. The one on the right-hand side is decorated with images of the Four Doctors of the Church, the coat of arms of the monastery and a matron representing Faith. The lamp, which serves to illuminate the Most Holy One, is the work of the Madrid silversmiths Nicolás Cervantes and Manuel García.

The Choir

Our itinerary culminates with the description of the Choir, the place reserved for the religious community. From the outset the choir constituted the nucleus around which the life of the Hieronymite monks revolved. Such was their vocation for the contemplative life that Philip II considered them the order most suitable to serve as the model for the liturgical reform carried out by the Council of Trent. The new order stipulated that they would remain daily in the temple for a minimum of eight hours and a maximum of fifteen, depending on the festivity celebrated that particular day. Besides the normal mass for that day, three masses were sung daily, prayers were said for the Hours and the Most Holy One, permanently displayed, was perpetually worshipped. In addition to this were the masses held for the birthdays and death anniversaries for all the dead buried in the pantheons, as well as for the rest of the Royal Family, the festivals corresponding to each liturgical period, those of the order, those of all the Spanish saints, especially the Archbishop of Toledo, and those of all the saints whose relics were preserved. The splendour of the cult was such that it was said that it surpassed even that of the Vatican. For this reason, the Choir evolved to the extent that it became a thoroughly differentiated place within the basilica.

Access to the choir is through the passages on the second floor, reached directly from the basilica by means of the Patronage Staircase. In the passages there are four altars, two on the left-hand side, of which only one still has its corresponding canvas, *The Vocation of St. Peter and St. Andrew* by Navarrete "el Mudo"; and two on the right-hand side, featuring *Jesus Christ and the Virgin Interceding on Behalf of the World before the Eternal Father* by Michel Coxcie and *St. Jerome at Prayer* by Nicolás Borrás.

Before reaching the choir we come to the antechoirs, of which we have spoken when referring to the decoration by Lucas Jordán. In these two large rooms is kept part of the choir bookshelves, which began to be installed here on August 8 1586. The collection consists of two hundred and sixteen choir books over one metre high, bound in calf leather and reinforced with bronze corner pieces. Each copy has two castors in order to make it easier to handle, due to its great weight. The illustration of these books constitutes one of the richest and most complete chapters in the art of miniatures in Spain from the XVI to the XVIII centuries.

The choir is fourteen metres wide by twenty-seven long and occupies the same space as the atrium. It is entered through two large semicircular arches after the antechoirs. Along the sides and the end wall are the one hundred and twenty-four seats on two levels that form the choir stalls. These were made by the Italian joiner Giuseppe Flecha after designs by Juan de Herrera. Outstanding here is the Prior's Chair, located on the end wall of the basilica and decorated with a XVI-century painting from the Italian school depicting *The Saviour*. Above, on the frontispiece there is a sculpture of St. Lawrence with his corresponding symbols: the grid and the book. In the right-hand corner of this wall is the chair of honour that Philip II occupied when he attended holy offices.

Above the elegant backs of the upper row of seats begins the pictorial decoration of the choir. At first the whole work was commissioned from Luca Cambiaso; however Philip II, unhappy with the work on the vault, also brought in Rómulo Cincinnato, who painted the stories on the side walls. One of the most ambitious projects here is the subject of *Glory*. It rep-

resents the triumph of the Holy Trinity over all the beings of Creation. This work completes the cycle of the main altar, whose last episode, *The Coronation of the Virgin by the Holy Trinity*, is also the work of Cambiasso. He began work in 1584 and, according to Father Sigüenza, completed it in fifteen months at grave risk to his health, due to "a posture so terribly uncomfortable and continual, in a vault where the body, head and arms were in a permanently contorted position and the artist was in contact with the cold and dampness of the plaster, water, lime and stucco, always so near." The fresco begins with the figures of God the Father and the Son, with the dove of the Holy Ghost, enthroned upon the rainbow within a halo of light and angels. His feet rest on a footstool in the form of a cube, which represents the Earth. On the sides are the Virgin Mary and St. John the Baptist, followed by the apostles and the evangelists. Next, in uniform, parallel rows which go from one side of the vault to the other appear all the hierarchies of saints, blessed ones, angels, seraphs, ancients, prophets, church fathers, martyrs, confessors, virgins, widows, children, popes and bishops, all sitting on benches of clouds. In the two lengthwise rows at the base of the vault were represented the earthly social strata, advised by the angels.

On the side walls, above the entrance arches, and on the end wall in rectangular niches with a golden background Cambiasso represented, in the form of large madonnas, the theological and cardinal virtues, together with the Church. On the left-hand side *Fortitude and Temperance* and *Prudence and Justice,* and on the right-hand side *Charity and Hope* and *Faith and the Church.* The end wall is completed with *The Annunciation,* beneath the semicircular arch and between the large window that illuminates the choir and, beneath the cornice, *St. Lawrence* and *St. Jerome.* On the organ sides Cambiasso continued with scenes from the lives of St. Lawrence and St. Jerome. The compositions were begun by this Genoan artist, but Philip II, tired of his sober style, ordered Rómulo Cincinnato to finish them. The episodes chosen were: *St. Jerome Writes his Commentaries on the Bible* and *St. Jerome Explains the Rule to his Monks;* opposite we see *St. Lawrence Goes out to Meet Pope Sixtus* and *St. Lawrence Shows the Roman Prefect the Treasures of the Church*.

In the centre of the choir was situated the magnificent rock crystal chandelier donated to the monastery by Charles II in 1676. The lamp, which was acquired by the Marquis of Astorga in Milan, depicts four peacocks with their tails open, and on the outer part an eagle with its wings extended resting on a globe. Although mutilated, the work still preserves its great beauty.

On the central axis we come across the large lectern designed by Juan de Herrera which, according to Father Sigüenza "is the biggest to be seen in Spain". It consists of four pillars of gilt bronze upon which the main body rests, in the form of a truncated pyramid crowned by a cornice and made of *ácana* wood reinforced with strips of gilt bronze. The lectern features a system of bars which allows it to rotate on its central axis. Above it appears a small temple in the form of a Greek cross crowned by a dome with a crucifix on top. Inside there is an image of the Virgin Mary attributed to Luiss Roldán.

Finally we must look at the organs, fundamental elements in liturgy since most of it was sung. In 1584 the monastery had four of these instruments, situated at both ends of the transept and on either side of the choir. These impressive machines were built by the Flemish brothers Giles and Michael Brebos (or Brevost) and their sound and variety of register were "a glory to hear", according to contemporary witnesses. Furthermore there were three *realejos* or small organs situated on three of the temple balconies, and thus it was possible to fill the whole of the basilica with music. After the fire of 1671, the organs were reconstructed by Pedro de Liborna Echeverría, including the typical horizontal exterior trumpetry, a characteristic element of Spanish baroque organs. The passing of the centuries and unfortunate modifications made it necessary in 1929 to pose the question of endowing San Lorenzo with a new set of instruments. This project was not brought to a conclusion until 1964, when the IV Centenary of the beginning of construction work on the monastery was held. The new instruments were built under the direction of Eusebio Soto and Ramón González Amezúa. From the central console, situated in the middle of the choir, it is possible to activate the four organs' over fifteen thousand pipes; it is also possible to play the transept organs individually, since they have their own consoles.

4. THE MONASTERY

Having taken the decision to found this monastery, Philip II had no doubts as to which religious order was to occupy it: the Brothers of St. Jerome. Thus, during the General Chapter held by this Order in the Monastery of Lupiana (Guadalajara) in 1561, the King requested the General that his order should take possession of the new residence. The religious community graciously obeyed the royal will, and immediately afterwards they proceeded to select the first prior, the privilege falling on Fray Juan de Huete.

The Order of St. Jerome is a phenomenon that emerged as the result of the religious reformist currents that developed in Europe during the XIV century. It was officially constituted in 1373, when Pope Gregory XI approved the cenobium constituted around the Monastery of San Bartolomé de Lupiana in Guadalajara with the name of "friars or hermits of St. Jerome", and proposed a new model of spiritual conduct, based on prayer and meditation on the Scriptures. Soon other communities also requested papal recognition, until the new Order was definitively constituted in a bull issued by Pope Benedict XIII in 1414, in which all the Hieronymite monasteries were brought under the authority of the Prior of Lupiana, accepting the rules of St. Augustin as the norm of conduct and with the faculty of holding chapters. This new form of religiosity had a strong impact on the Castilian upper classes who, weary of the easy life at court and disenchanted by the corruption that was rife at the time among the clergy, accepted this way of life with great enthusiasm. During the reign of John I of Castile, the Hieronymite monks were invited to settle in the Monastery of Guadalupe, of which they took possession on October 22 1389. They soon achieved royal favour by virtue of their great abnegation, the noble origin of most of the members and their purely Castilian nature.

The Order of St. Jerome grew rapidly and, between 1373 and 1516, forty-five monasteries and four convents were founded, followed by nine more between 1516 and 1835, the year in which the order was dissolved. As I explain above, their success was based on the imposition of a severe life style devoted to prayer and study; furthermore, unlike in the case of Franciscans and Carthusians, this life was open to laymen, either for a short period or for the rest of their lives. It was this possibility of leading a monk's life without having to take any vows that so attracted the Castilian aristocracy.

The House of Austria upheld the prerogatives of the Hieronymites, who attained their highest splendour when the Emperor Charles V chose a Hieronymite cenobium, the Monastery of Yuste, in which to retire after his abdication in 1555. Consequently, Philip II's choice was the confirmation of the tight links between this order and the Spanish Royal Family.

From its origins the Hieronymite Order was arranged in a way characteristic of the architectural layout of the monastery, which demanded the creation of a group of patios sufficient in number to provide room for all the cells, since these consisted of several rooms, and to create at the same time wide thoroughfares for the processions held inside the building. The layout of San Lorenzo is a perfect combination of the demands of a Hieronymite monastery and the royal prerogatives that converted the building into the House of the King of Spain. To achieve this the monks called upon the services of the master builder Brother Antonio de Villacastín, a figure half way between the architect and the different craftsmen (stonemasons, bricklayers, carpenters, transporters and suppliers of material and tools) who ensured that the norms were fully satisfied.

Within the layout of the building, the church with its atrium forms the axis around which the remainder of the dependencies revolve, following the patterns on which, beginning with the Monastery of St. Gallen, all Christian cenobia have been based. On the southern side, the monastery has room for two hundred monks, while on the northern side the residence for the Monarch and his family is, in the case of San Lorenzo, arranged around the head wall of the temple, the royal alcove being aligned with the rest of the cells.

The monastery is arranged around a great courtyard, known as the *Claustro Principal* (Main Cloister) and four

smaller ones, here known as the *claustros menores* (lesser cloisters); thus there is a total of five, unlike other Hieronymite
foundations, which usually have two or three. The main cloister is the axis around which the monks' lives revolved, and it
was considered the extension of the sacred place of the
temple. Consequently, the law of silence had to be obeyed
here also. One of its most important uses was as a place of burial for the community. However, in the case of San Lorenzo
this Hieronymite custom was altered substantially, since this
patio was used exclusively as a thoroughfare for processions,
the cemetery being transferred to one of the smaller cloisters.
Furthermore, the distribution of the dependencies differs
from the standard model, since at the lower end of this cloister we find the sacristy, the prior's cell, the capitular rooms,
the private church, the main staircase and the lodge, the remaining cells being arranged on the second floor and in the
two adjacent lesser cloisters. The other two cloisters were
used to house the administrative offices, the hospice and the
monks'infirmary.

Today, visits to the monastery are limited to the dependencies situated in the Lower Main Cloister, that is, the *Sala de
la Trinidad,* the Main Staircase, the Capitular Halls, and the
Lower Prior's Cell. The Sacristy and the private church are
still used by the present community and are opened to the
public only on special occasions.

The Sala de la Trinidad

The main entrance to the monastery is in the *Patio de Reyes,*
in the entrance portico to the church, on the right-hand
side. After passing through a small hall, known as the *Sala de
los Secretos* (Hall of Secrets) by virtue of its special acoustics
which make it possible for two people to whisper to each
other from opposite corners, we reach the lodge, in descriptions of the time called the *recibo* or *parlatorio.* This large hall,
of over sixteen metres long by almost ten wide, has since the
mid XIX century been called the *Sala de la Trinidad* (Hall of the

Trinity) because of the painting which hangs over the mantel-piece which presides it. This room leads into the main cloister through a wide, two-leafed door, and into one of the smaller ones, known as the *claustro del convento,* through two narrower ones. The only furniture here is a long, high-backed walnut bench made at the end of the XVI century, on which guests could sit.

Decoration

The most important work preserved here, and which gives the hall its name, is a canvas by the Spanish painter José de Ribera entitled *La Santísima Trinidad* (the Holy Trinity) painted around 1635. Following a composition in which diagonally curved lines predominate, Ribera presents us with one of the most human versions of this dogma of the Catholic Church. All the emotional tension is concentrated in the expression of God the Father on the point of resting his hand on the head of the dead body of his Son.

Also outstanding are three copies of Bassano which illustrate episodes in the life of Noah: *The Building of the Ark*, *The Animals Boarding the Ark* and *Noah after the Flood*.

The Lower Main Cloister

The Order of St. Jerome, being a community who led a contemplative life, endowed their cloisters with rich decoration since they were considered an extension of the holy church and, consequently, places for prayer and meditation as well as thoroughfares for processions. Construction of the main cloister did not begin until 1569, when the underground cistern was installed to serve the lavatories in the ante-sacristy. Although the plans for the cloister are by Juan Bautista de Toledo, they were actually executed by Juan de Herrera, who altered the project, endowing it with greater articulation and elegance, by including the pedestal from which all the interior pilasters stem.

Mural Paintings

This part of the monastery was from the very outset endowed with a careful selection of paintings, arranged throughout the cloister and up the main staircase. The project was begun by Luca Cambiaso, by whom only two stations of the cross are preserved, but since the work of this artist was not to Philip II's liking, he was substituted by Pellegrino Tibaldi. The vast work was carried out by this master who, assisted by his studio, developed to the maximum his "pointillist" miniature technique, the traces of which the inclemencies of the weather and the restorations it has undergone have almost completely obliterated. Work began in 1586 and five years went by until this impressively ambitious programme was completed, depicting in a grandiose style using large figures in extensive architectural spaces the *Story of the Salvation from the Conception of the Virgin Mary to the Final Judgment*.

In this way the iconographical programme of the main altar was completed, showing the most important moments of this Singular History, consisting of sixty-two scenes of which Tibaldi and his studio produced thirty-six, corresponding almost entirely to the frescoes. On the staircase we find two stations of the cross of the five by Luca Cambiaso, since Philip II ordered Tibaldi to repaint the other three, which he considered to be of low quality. The four corners of this hall acquire greater importance in that each of them contains one of the most relevant moments in the life of Jesus Christ. For this reason, instead of being painted they were substituted by wooden triptychs by Luis de Carvajal, Miguel Barroso, Rómulo Cincinnato and Tibaldi himself. These triptychs are opened only during the processions. The subject we see when the doors are closed is the same that appears when they are opened, except that the composition differs.

Description

We begin our itinerary at the northern end of the cloister, on our right when facing the Processions Gate:

Northern Side:

1. The Conception of Mary or the Encounter with the Golden Gate.
2. The Nativity of the Virgin Mary.
3. The Presentation of the Virgin in the Temple.
4. The Nuptials of the Virgin Mary and St. Joseph.
5. The Annunciation.
6. The Visitation.
7. The Angel Appears before the Shepherds.
8. Triptych: The Birth of Jesus Christ and the Adoration of the Shepherds, by Luis de Carvajal.
9. The Circumcision.

Eastern Side:

10. The Baptism.
11. Triptych: The Adoration of the Wise Men, by Luis de Carvajal.
12. The Weddings of Canaan.
13. The Presentation of Christ in the Temple or the Purification of the Virgin.
14. The Flight into Egypt.
15. The Slaughter of the Innocents.
16. The Return to Egypt.
17. The Child Lost and Found in the Temple.
18. The Temptations in the Wilderness.
19. The Choice of the Apostles.
20. The Resurrection of Lazarus.
21. The Expulsion of the Merchants from the Temple.
22. Christ and the Samaritan.
23. Triptych: The Transfiguration, by Rómulo Cincinnato.
24. Christ and the Adulteress.

Southern Side:

25. The Entry into Jerusalem.
26. Triptych: The Last Supper, by Rómulo Cincinnato.
27. The Lavatory.
28. The Prayer in the Garden.
29. The Arrest of Jesus Christ.
30. Christ before **Anás**.
31. Christ before Caiaphas.
32. Christ before Herod.
33. The Flagellation.
34. The Crown of Thorns.
35. Ecce-Homo.
36. Pilate Washes his Hands.

Open triptychs of the "Crucifixion" and the "Resurrection of Christ" by Tibaldi.

37. The Departure of Christ, Bearing the Cross, through the Gate of Jerusalem.
38. Christ in Nailed to the Cross.
39. Triptych: The Crucifixion, by Tibaldi.
40. The Descent.

Western Side:
41. The Burial of Christ.
42. Triptych: The Resurrection, by Tibaldi.
43. Christ Descends into Limbo.
44. Christ Appears to His Mother.
45. The Women beside the Empty Tomb.

Staircase:
46. St. Peter and St. John beside the Empty Tomb, by Cambiasso.
47. Noli me Tangere.
48. Christ Appears before the Holy Women.
49. The Path to **Emaus**.
50. Christ Appears before the Disciples in the Hall of the Eucharist, by Cambiasso.

Western Side:
51. The Doubt of St. Thomas.
52. The Miraculous Catch.
53. Christ Appears to His Disciples.
54. Triptych: The Ascent, by Miguel Barroso.
55. Christ Appears to His Disciples.

Northern Side:
56. St. Peter Preaching.
57. Triptych: The Pentecost, by Miguel Barroso.
58. The Placing of the Hands on the Believers.
59. The Passing of the Virgin.
60. Mary's Ascent into Heaven.
61. The Coronation of the Virgin.
62. The Last Judgment.

The Main Staircase

T he main staircase is situated in the centre of the western bay of the cloister, occupying a total of three arches, and links the two floors forming this part of the monastery. It is in the "imperial" style, that is, two flights go from the ground floor to the large landing, and then make an about-turn, becoming divided into two parallel ramps also in two flights which finally reach the floor above. The staircase well juts outwards in the form of an oblong tower covered with a garret-like roof featuring a set of windows which provide light not only for this section but also for the adjoining corridors. Such an important project was entrusted first to the Italian architect Giambattista Castello, called El Bergamasco, who presented it to the king in 1567. The plans could not have been to the monarch's liking, however, for Philip II ordered the staircase to be constructed following his own instructions and according to plans by Juan de Herrera.

Vault

We do not know whether in the initial project for the staircase there was any intention to decorate the vault with the stations of the cross as on the walls of the well and in the lower cloister. The only in formation we have concerning this is that provided by Father Sigüenza, who informs us that it was stuccoed like those of the basilica. Its present-day decoration was commissioned by Charles II from the Neapolitan painter Lucas Jordán as part of the programme of improvements carried out by this monarch after the fire of 1671. The artist completed his task between 1692 and 1693, following the iconographical indications of Father Francisco de los Santos, at that time prior of the monastery, and of the king himself. The subjects chosen were *The Battle of San Quintín* and *The Construction of the Monastery of San Lorenzo* for the frieze below the vault, and *The Glory of the House of Austria*.

Frieze

The Battle of San Quintín occupies three sides of the stair well and begins on the southern wall where the assault which culminated in the capture of the city is depicted. We see the moment when, after the rout of the French troops, prisoners are taken, including Connétable Montmorency and his son. Following onto the western wall we se the Spanish forces before the walls of San Quintín, and finally on the north wall the moment when the victorious soldiers lead the captured defender of the city, the Admiral of France, to Manuel Filiberto, Duke of Savoy. Behind stand the Spanish soldiers carrying the banners taken from the enemy. *The Construction of the Monastery of San Lorenzo,* on the eastern side of the frieze, describes the beginning of the work. To our right we find Philip II, accompanied by his jester, Miguel de Antoña, before the architects Juan Bautista de Toledo and Juan de Hererra who, together with Fray Antonio de Villacastín, discuss the plans for the building. On one side appear workmen laying the foundations. This is one of the oldest representations, in which the Battle of San Quintín is related to the foundation of the Monastery of San Lorenzo.

The work seems to have been painted on canvas fixed to the wall by a golden frame. This, however, is a trick on the part of the painter, which acquires all its force with the apparently torn pieces of canvas.

Vault

The vault begins above fourteen windows at the side of which angels bear blazons with the coat of arms of the Spanish Empire. Above the lunettes, in the form of medallions imitating porphyry, appear further war scenes which tell of the invincible military power of the House of Austria. In the central lunette to the west we find the portrait of Charles II and on the opposite side that of Philip IV.

As we climb the stairs, at the base of the vault we see King Charles II in the company of his second wife, Marian of Neoburg, and his mother, Queen Marian of Austria, who contemplate from a balustrade *The Glory of the House of Austria*. The choice of this subject and its execution reveals the personality of the last king of this dynasty who, perfectly aware that with his death the lineage would come to an end, presents to his wife and mother the greatness of his most illustrious forebears: Charles I and Philip II. The idea was not a new one, since we see how Lucas Jordán has synthesised in this composition paintings which at the time hung in the monastery. I refer first of all to Titian's *Glory,* now in the Prado Museum, but which during the XVII century hung in the *Aula de Moral* (Morals Classroom) of this building. The second work is the *Glory* by Cambiasso which, as we have seen, is in the temple choir. Finally we see El Greco's *Adoration of the Name of Jesus* which now hangs in the chapter halls.

The centre of the composition is the Holy Trinity, from which emanates the light which illuminates the scene; to their right, enveloped in a blue cloak, is the Virgin Mary as the first intercessor on behalf of humanity, accompanied by a group of angels who bear all the elements of the Passion. Beneath God the Father appears a group of crowned and cloaked figures representing the saint kings: St. Hermenegild and St. Ferdinand of Spain; St. Henry, Emperor of Germany; St. Eusebius, King of Hungary; and St. Casimir, Prince of Poland. Beneath these two groups we find the intercessor saints of the Hispanic Monarchy: to our left, the kneeling figure of St. Lawrence, dressed in a fine red dalmatic, who points towards our right, where Charles V, also kneeling, offers the Crown of Spain and the Imperial Crown, followed by Philip II, also kneeling, with the orb in his hands. Above them, in the red cardinal's habit, St. Jerome points to the sovereigns, on behalf of whom he intercedes. On either side of these figures appear two matrons who symbolise the Royal Majesty (left) and the Catholic Church (right). the group is completed in the four corners by the Cardinal Virtues.

The theme is treated with all the richness and vigour of the Baroque, which harmonises admirably with the severity of the building.

The Patio de los Evangelistas

When Father Sigüenza speaks of this courtyard he says that he imagines it as a mystical earthly paradise by virtue of its great beauty and harmony, and completes his description by saying: "If we pay heed to what we bear in our soul we would never leave this great cloister; but leave we must, even if it is by flying over the roofs".

The area created around the main cloister is called the *Patio de los Evangelistas* (Patio of the Evangelists) because of the sculptures in the small central templet. The execution of this project, designed by Juan Bautista de Toledo and re- alised, with certain variations, by Juan de Herrera, is one of this building's major lessons in architecture. What strikes the visitor most is the richness of its decoration, in which every detail is a technical tour-de-force, which contrasts with the basilica, one side of which is visible, the epitome of the unadorned severity of the monastery's predominant style. On each side of the patio there are eleven arches which form two storeys and are Doric with base on the first and Ionic on the second. The whole structure is surrounded by a balustrade which maintains the rhythm marked by the arches thanks to plinths which coincide with the pillars, crowned with balls of granite, a decorative element re- peated throughout the building.

In the centre of the patio stands the templet which, as a kind of *Fons Vitae* (Fountain of Life), speaks of a complex iconographical programme in which the message of the Gospel is compared to water, without which there is no life. The layout of the construction follows that of the dome, the number of vanes being reduced to four and the pillars used to create large niches in which the sculptures are housed. We have already seen this model in the tabernacle of the

church. The whole complex is in granite and the interior is lined in different coloured marble and jasper. In the tradition of Spanish monasteries it is normal to find this kind of construction in the centre of the main cloister; for this reason we need not be surprised to find it in San Lorenzo, and there is no need to justify its presence in terms of foreign influences.

The iconographical programme was proposed by Father Sigüenza, who conceived the patio as the Garden of Eden from which the four rivers flow (the Pisón, the Tigris, the Euphrates and the Guijón) which irrigated the four parts of the world then known (Asia, Africa, Europe and America). This patio can also be interpreted in a political way, since Philip II's domains extended over the whole globe and in all of them the faith of the Catholic Church was preached. The templet represents Jesus Christ, fountain and principle of life, who transmits his doctrine -symbolised by the water- over the whole world through the Word, contained in the Gospels and spread by the Apostles. The patio is divided into four large squares, oriented towards the cardinal points, which in turn are subdivided into a further four. Thus sixteen areas are created: the four surrounding the templet are ponds and the remaining twelve are landscaped areas. In this way allusions are made to the Evangelists and the Apostles.

The sculptures are in four groups representing the Evangelists and their symbols. The work was entrusted to the Toledan Juan Bautista Monegro in 1589, and it took him five years to complete his task. The sculptures were finally placed in their respective niches on May 15 1593. Each Evangelist is made from a single block of marble and is slightly over one metre seventy centimetres tall. All the figures are dressed in elegant tunics and carry an open book in which it is possible to read a fragment of their Gospel, written in the original language and with a Latin translation. The group is arranged as follows:

- St. Matthew, accompanied by an angel, shows us two leaves, one in Latin and the other in Hebrew, which say "Go and teach the people, baptising them in the name of the Father, the Son and the Holy Ghost".

- St. Luke accompanied by a bull; his book, written in Greek and Latin, says "I baptise you with water; another will come who is stronger than I; he will baptise you with the Holy Spirit and with fire".

- St. Mark, next to the lion, presents two leaves written in Latin which, translated, say "He who believes and is baptised shall be saved; he who does not believe shall be condemned. The signs that the believes will bear are these, in my name the devils will be expelled...".

- St. John, who curiously enough is here bearded, presents his Gospel written in Latin and Syrian. At his feet we see an eagle. His text says "In truth I say unto you that he who is not reborn by water and the Holy Spirit cannot enter the Kingdom of God".

After the fire of 1671, it was decided to replace the original flowering plants, which provided the patio with a greater colour display, with boxwood hedges very similar to the ones we see today.

The Old Church

In 1571 the southern section of the complex, today the part corresponding to the monastery itself, was considered complete, and the Hieronymite community were able to settle into their new home. This first finished section had to house the monks, the King and the court, and the first six royal corpses which had been brought from the Monastery of Yuste and from Madrid. As the church had not yet been begun, a large area had to be furbished so that all religious ceremonies could be held there, and which would also serve as the Royal Pantheon. This was the place chosen, and for this reason was called the *Iglesia del prestado*. When work on the basilica was completed (1585), all official liturgical activity was transferred to the new building and this original dependency was kept exclusively for the private use of the monks, becoming known, for this reason, as the *Iglesia Vieja* (Old Church). Today the Old Church continues to perform the same function for the Augustinian Order.

The chapel consists of a nave almost thirty metres long by ten wide, and is divided into three sections by projecting stone arches. Through a wide two-leafed door, the church opens into the lower main cloister, which forms a pair with the *Patio de la Trinidad;* and through two smaller ones into the *Claustro de Difuntos* (Cloister of the Deceased). Its current decoration is in no way reminiscent of its original use, since his was at first the residence of King Philip II. After the initial phase of the construction of the monastery, the king realised that in order for work to be speeded up, what had already been finished had to be put to use. For this reason, as soon as the first phase of the operation had been concluded, he decided that the Hieronymites should begin to use it, as a way of urging on the builders in their work. With this decision the ceremonial complex was put to the test which had to regulate the life of San Lorenzo. The brothers occupied the area around the minor cloisters; the king, together with his deceased family members, the *Iglesia del prestado;* and the court the chapter rooms, which thus became the centre of daily affairs. This part of the building originally had five doors: two of them, those which linked the royal residence to the chapter rooms and the *Claustro de Difuntos*, have since disappeared. In the first section the royal room was prepared and, above it, the choir, destined for the monks. The central section was reserved for the court and in the last section two levels were built: the first, known as the vault, became the Royal Pantheon and the second, the Main Altar. The original decoration consisted only of sixteen tapestries from the royal collection.

When work on the building was completed, it was decided to turn this church into a chapel; the king's residence, the choir and the staircase leading down into the vault were therefore removed, leaving the area open. The walls and the ceiling were plastered, the floor paved with white and brown marble flagstones and the seating was adapted to its new use. Only the three presbytery altars, decorated with paintings by

Titian, were left untouched, since the tapestries were returned to the royal collection. During the reign of Philip IV the presbytery was renovated, the original altars being replaced by the present ones, made from jasper. The altar paintings remained, and the number of canvases on the walls was increased.

The main altar today is exactly as it was in the XVII century, with its set of paintings by Titian depicting *The Martyrdom of St. Lawrence*. This canvas, painted between 1554 and 1567, was conceived by the Venetian master to decorate the main altar of the basilica. Although the king was thoroughly satisfied with the painting, it was never placed in the position for which it was commissioned, possibly because it would not have been properly visible there. The work, inspired in a composition Titian had done ten years earlier for the Jesuits of Venice, reveals the moment when St. Lawrence sees a shining light in the sky as a divine sign of acceptance of his martyrdom. The painting, one of the masterpieces of the Italian Renaissance, is a clear example of the plenitude of style of the later years of this Venetian artist, who applied a technique based on pigments highly charged with oil, which endow the painting with its extraordinary texture and light effects.

On the side altars we can contemplate, on the left-hand side, *The Adoration of the Three Kings* and, on the right-hand side, *The Holy Burial*, a later copy whose original is in the Prado Museum, although it was originally here. Above these two canvases we find copies of a *Dolorosa* and an *Ecce Homo*, he originals for which are by this Venetian master.

In the following section of the chapel we find two paintings attributed to the Spanish painter José de Ribera, known as "El Españoleto" representing the same subject, *The Adoration of the Shepherds*. Although both paintings are of great quality, today they are considered to have been produced largely by Ribera's workshop with Juan Do, one of his Spanish pupils, at the forefront.

It would be impossible to conclude this description without mentioning the carpentry of this room. In the first place the sober seating with its prominent prior's chair, on the frontis-

Old Church with "The Martyrdom of St. Lawrence" by Titian.

piece of which appears a canvas by the Venetian School of the XVI century, depicting Jesus Christ bearing the Cross. The decoration is completed on the side backs with the figures of St. Jerome and St. Lawrence sculpted in bas-relief. In the second place, attention must be drawn to the marquetry door that opens into the *Claustro de Difuntos.*

The old church is used today by the Military Order of St. Hermenegild and St. Ferdinand, who hold their chapter here every two years. For this reason on either side of the prior's chair there are square cloths bearing their coat of arms and symbols.

The Chapter Rooms

Like all religious foundations, the Monastery of San Lorenzo has a special area set aside for the community to discuss internal issues and to examine the strict observance of the rules or norms that govern life in the cenobium. This area receives the name of chapter, since all the meetings held here begin with a reading from one of the chapters of the Holy Scriptures. The new and complex organisation of this monastery -due to the considerable number of monks and the high authority bestowed upon the prior- made it necessary to create two chapters, known respectively as the *Capítulo Prioral* and the *Capítulo Vicarial.*

The chapter rooms occupy the southern end of the lower main cloister, and they are reached through a large vestibule, situated in the centre and coinciding with the axis of the Templet of the Evangelists. The visit to this dependency includes the prior's lower cell, which leads into the *Capítulo Prioral.* The decoration of the halls corresponds to the arrangement imposed after the celebration of the IV centenary of the completion of the building, when it was decided that only paintings would be hung in order to come as close as possible to the decoration they had in the XVII century. This decorative programme was prepared by Diego de Velázquez who, on Philip IV's orders, brought to San Lorenzo the most import-

ant religious paintings in the royal collections. The ups and downs which the monastery has suffered through time have made it impossible for this reconstruction to be made in its totality; for this reason, and having as our main idea the criteria followed by Velázquez, we have decided to pinpoint the most significant works.

Vestibule

In the atrium or vestibule of the chapters Spanish paintings from the XVI and XVII centuries are exhibited:

1.- *The Mystical Nuptials of St. Catherine and St. Sebastian*, a copy of the original by Antonio Allegri, "Il Correggio", traditionally attributed to El Greco.

2.- *Noli me Tangere*, Alonso Sánchez Coello's copy of a lost work by Titian (of which only the head of Christ is still preserved).

3.- *St. John the Baptist*, and

4. *St. John the Evangelist*, both from the XVII-century Spanish School.The ceiling decoration is the only original element remaining in this hall, and is the work of brothers Fabrizio Castello and Nicolás Granello, Lázaro Tavarón and Orazio Cambiasso in the "grotto" style, so-called because it imitates the kind of Roman painting found during excavations of the *Domus Aurea* or Palace of Emperor Nero.

Capítulo Vicarial

This hall contains mostly Spanish painting from the XVI and XVII centuries. Our description begins on the walls running lengthwise:

1.- *St. Onofre, the Hermit*, by José de Ribera. It depicts the kneeling hermit delivering his soul to God. The work was produced in 1639 in collaboration with the painter's workshop.

2.- *The Holy Burial,* copy of a work by Ribera. The painting shows the moment when the lifeless body of Christ is placed in the shroud.

3.- *Jacob Receives Joseph's Tunic,* by Diego de Velázquez (known as *Joseph's Tunic*). The painting shows the moment in the story of Joseph in which his brothers present to their aged father the tunic he had given his son as a gift, stained with the blood of a billy goat. Jacob, his face contorted with grief, recognises his son's garment and believes he has been devoured by a savage beast. The expressions of complicity on his sons' faces could not be more significant, in contrast to their father's despair. This work was produced during the painter's first trip to Italy between 1629 and 1630.

4.- *Jacob Guarding the Flock of Laban,* the original by José de Ribera. This canvas, painted in 1630, marks the beginning of the maturity of this artist, when his composition became simple but full of visual effects, as we can see here in the figure of Jacob.

5.- *St. Francis of Assisi in Ecstasy,* a work of great quality by Ribera's studio.

6.- *St. Peter* by El Greco. This painting, together with its partner, *St. Eugene*, were produced for the Church of San Vicente in Toledo between 1610 and 1614. They are mentioned as being in San Lorenzo for the first time in Father Santos' description.

7.- *St. Francis at Prayer*, an original, signed and dated in 1590, by El Greco.

8.- *Allegory of the Holy League and Adoration of the Name of Jesus*, otherwise known as *The Dream of Philip II*, by El Greco. In the foreground we see Philip II dressed in black and kneeling in an attitude of prayer, accompanied by Pope Pius V, the Duce of Venice, Alvise Mocenigo and, with his hands resting on a sword, Don John of Austria. The group is between Hell -represented by a great monster that devours the condemned- and the just, in attitude of prayer. At the top, and surrounded by angels, appears Christ's monogram (IHS), giving meaning to the composition inspired in the words of St. Paul: "so that before the Name of Jesus shall kneel all creatures in Heaven, on Earth and in the Subterranean Regions". The work was painted between 1577 and 1579, possibly to celebrate the victory of Lepanto.

9.- *St. John the Evangelist and St. John the Baptist*, the work of a

XVII-century Spanish artist.

10.- *St. Francis of Assisi,* the work of El Greco's studio.

11.- *St. Eugene, Bishop of Toledo* by El Greco. Comparing this painting and its partner (*St. Peter*) with *"The Dream of Philip II"*, we notice a much looser and freer brushstroke which, on the basis of light effects, gives form to the figures.

12.- *St. Jerome at Prayer* by Titian. This canvas was sent to Philip II at the end of 1575 to decorate the same altar on which it can still be admired today. It may have been painted around 1560 and retouched by the master before being sent to Spain. The saint appears kneeling on a crag before a crucifix beating himself on the breast with a stone, an example of Christian piety for the Hieronymite community.

On the shorter sides of the chapter room we find four works from Ribera's studio, representing

13. *St. Jerome* and

14.- *St. Paul the Hermit* at the sides of the altar,

15.- *St. John the Baptist as a Child, Laughing* and

16. *St. Jerome.*

Above the doors there is a series of four garlands of flowers inside each of which there is a scene from the Old Testament. The floral adornment of the composition is by Mario Nuzzi, known as "Mario dei Fiori", while the biblical scene is attributed to an unidentified artist from Rome. The chosen subjects are:

17.- *Cain Slaying Abel* and

18.- *Moses Receiving the Tablets of the Law,* as the visitor enters, and

19.- *Jacob's Dream* and

20.- *The Sacrifice of Isaac* at the sides of the altar.

"The Adoration of the Name of Jesus", by El Greco.

The ceiling decoration in the "grotto" style is by a team of Genoese artists, Fabrizio Castello, Nicolás Granello, Lanzarón Tavarón and Orazio Cambiasso, the latter being responsible for the vestibule. On the short sides of the ceiling are porphyry altars representing *The Virgin Mary with the Child Jesus* and *The Saviour*. These interesting pieces were donated to the monastery by the king, together with those in the *Capítulo Prioral*, and were probably brought from Italy by Pompeius Leoni.

In the centre of the hall there is a lectern in the form of an eagle with wings outstretched, created by Simón de Amberes (Simon of Antwerp) in 1571 in order for the Gospel According to St. John to be read from it.

Capítulo Prioral

This hall is devoted mainly to XVI-century Venetian painting. Our description begins along the walls that run lengthwise:

1.- *Rest During the Flight to Egypt,* a work produced in Titian's studio around 1536 which entered the monastery during the reign of Philip IV. Along with the Holy Family we see St. Isabelle and St. John who, according to the Apocryphal Gospel, also fled to Egypt.

2.- *The Conversion of Magdalene* by Jacopo Tintoretto, who produced the work between 1546 and 1547 assisted considerably by his studio. The canvas describes the moment when Mary Magdalene prepares to anoint Christ's feet, to the astonishment of the onlookers.

3.- *The Last Supper,* which Philip II commissioned Titian to paint in 1563 for the monastery refectory, marking a clear parallel between this work and Leonardo da Vinci's fresco for the refectory of the Convent of Santa María de las Gracias. The chosen moment is the one when Christ utters the terrible words "One of you will betray me", giving scope for the interplay of gestures and movements of the apostles who look at and point to each other, wondering who it will be. The painting was cut at the top and at the sides in order to fit the wall where it was to hang.

4.- *Queen Esther before King Asuero,* painted by Jacopo Tintoretto in 1547 with the help of his studio. The canvas depicts the moment when the queen faints to the surprise of Asuero, since his wife had appeared without being summoned.

5.- *Apparition of Jesus Christ before His Mother, Accompanied by the Souls in Purgatory,* attributed to Veronese. According to Christian tradition, after his resurrection Christ first appeared to His mother, the Virgin Mary.

6.- *The Burial of Christ,* attributed to Domenico Tintoretto.

7.- *Ecce Homo,* copy of an original by Titian, now lost.

8.- *Jesus Christ is Presented to the People by Pilate,* produced by Titian's studio around 1580.

9.- *Christ and the Samaritan Woman,* attributed to Paolo Veronese and painted around 1580.

10.- *The Holy Family with St. John as a Child,* by the studio of Carletto Veronese.

11.- *St. John the Baptist* by Titian, painted around 1560. The saint appears as the precursor of the Messiah, holding a parchment that says, in Latin, "Here is the Lamb of God".

12.- *The Prayer in the Garden* by Titian. The work was painted around 1560 and reached Spain in 1562. It was destined to preside over the altar in this chapter room.

At the sides of the altar we find two canvases (nos. 13 and 14) by Moretto da Brescia, depicting *The Prophet Isiah* and *The Eritrean Sibyl.*

As we enter the hall we find a further pair of canvases, these by the XVI-century Flemish school:

15.- *The Resurrection of Jesus Christ* and

16.- *Jesus Christ Saving the Souls of the Just from Limbo.*

Finally, above the doors there is a set of four canvases by the Flemish painter Daniel Seghers, who using a garland of flowers as a frame develops the following themes:

17.- *The Virgin Mary and the Child Jesus, Holding the Globe* and

18.- *The Virgin Mary with the Child Jesus and an Angel Offering Him the Cross,* as the visitor enters, and

19.- *The Virgin with Attributes of Passion*

20.- *The Virgin with the Child Jesus Asleep.*

The ceiling was decorated, also in the "grotto" style, by the same team of Genoese artists who did that of the *Capítulo Vicarial.* On the short sides appear two porphyry altars depicting *The Virgin Mary with the Child Jesus* and *The Saviour,* produced probably in Florence.

In the centre of the hall there is a lectern in the form of an angel from which to read the Gospel According to St. Matthew. The gilt bronze statue was made by Simon of Antwerp in 1571.

The Prior's Lower Cell

Next on our itinerary is the largest room of the prior's summer cell, the so-called Prior's Tower with windows looking south and east. Still preserved from the original decoration is the impressive ceiling, which was created by Francesco de Urbino in collaboration with his brother Juan María and Nicolás Granello. In the centre of the composition there is a *Solomon's Judgment.* The room is given over to Flemish painter, and mainly to Hieronymus Bosch, one of Philip II's favourite artists.

1.- *The Ascent to Calvary,* a panel which Bosch painted around 1507. The composition depicts the moment when Christ is helped to carry the Cross by Simon the Cyrenean.

2.- *The Hay Cart,* a triptych by Bosch inspired in the words of Isiah:

"All flesh is grass and all splendour like the flowers of the mea-
dow". The work is considered to be a copy of the original which
is in the Prado Museum and which was also the property of Philip II. On the door to our left appears the creation of Eve, the original sin and the expulsion from Eden; in the centre, the future of
human life that places all its hopes on ephemeral things, symbolised by the hay cart; and on the door to our right, Hell with some
of its punishments. The triptych is in fact the Story of Humanity.

3.- *The Creation,* a copy of the right-hand panel of Bosch's *Garden
of Delights*.

4.- *The Crown of Thorns,* an original panel by Bosch painted
around 1510. According to Father Sigüenza, this work "shows the
envy and rage of false wisdom, which does not rest until it takes
the life of innocence, which is Christ".

5.- *The Miracle of the Loaves and Fishes* by the school of the Flemish
painter Joachim Patinir.

6.- *The Temptations of St. Anthony,* the copy of a painting by Bosch,
made in the monastery itself. The feminine figure originally
tempting the saint has been replaced by a crucifix.

7.- *The Temptations of St. Anthony* by Bosch's school.

8.- *The Temptations of St. Anthony*. This panel is considered to be a
XVI-century copy of an original Dutch work painted in the previous century.

9.- *The Temptations of St. Anthony* by the Dutch painter and engraver Peter Huys.

Presiding over the altar in this cell is the *Altarpiece or Portable Altar of Charles V,* made in gilt silver, enamel and wood
during the first half of the XVI century. The work was donated to San Lorenzo in 1567.

The frontal of this altar is a porphyry and silver piece made
in the second half of the XVII century by the monks Eugenio
de la Cruz and Juan de la Concepción for the chapel of the
Virgin of Patronage.

"The Crown of Thorns", by Bosch.

The Ante-Sacristy.

The Sacristy

Situated on the eastern side of the building, the Sacristy occupies this whole side of the cloister. At the moment it cannot be visited since it is still in use. We must not forget that the Monastery of San Lorenzo is a living entity and that it continues to fulfil the same functions as those for which it was destined by its founder over four hundred years ago. One of these, perhaps the most important, is religious worship, for which the sacristy is necessary as the place where the celebrants change their vestments and where all the objects for divine ceremonies are kept.

The ante-sacristy

The ante-sacristy is reached either from the cloister or from the basilica through the chapel where the altar of the

General view of the Sacristy.

Virgin of Patronage originally was. This large square room serves as the entrance hall to the sacristy and contains the impressive font which the priests used to wash before beginning the religious rites. The only painted decoration is on the ceiling and is by Nicolás Granello and Fabrizio Castello. In the centre of the composition, in a patch of sky, an angel appears bearing a pitcher and towels, symbols of the ceremonial washing.

Hanging on the walls are thirteen paintings depicting the pontifical concessions and indulgences that can be gained in this basilica. Beneath these is a long, high-backed walnut bench which in its day also served as a wardrobe.

The most important work preserved here is the font, made from a single block of brown marble. It has six gilt bronze spouts in the form of angels' heads.

The Sacristy

The sacristy of San Lorenzo is included the major icono-graphical programme begun in the main cloister and in the chapter rooms. Its situation could be considered strategic, since it is linked to all the most relevant areas of the building. The sacristy has changed little since the XVI century, the only modification being the Altar of the Sacred Form, which was built on the end wall late in the XVII century. Consequently, Father Sigüenza's words are still valid when he writes "When entering through the sacristy door the visitor's heart rejoices on seeing a room so great, so clear, so beautiful, so full of such a variety of divine things, of such composure, richness, clean-liness, the product of hands and diligence more than human, and then one sees that it is purely the changing room of the House of God".

A considerable number of elements of the original decora-tion are still preserved, such as the impressive chest of dra-wers backed against the wall, in which liturgical ornaments and cult objects are kept. This piece of furniture was made from fine inlaid and mosaic wood and consists of two orders: the first with large drawers provided with castors so that they may be opened with greater ease, and the second, with cup-boards in the form of larders. The only adornment here takes the form of seven baroque mirrors outstanding among which is the one in the middle, by virtue of its complex decoration. It was a gift from Queen Marian of Austria.

The ceiling was decorated by the same Genoese artists who did those of the chapter rooms. The "grotto" style applied here is simpler, and geometrical elements predominate over figurative ones.

The most important canvas here is Titian's *Christ Crucified,* painted in 1565, which has presided over the sacristy since the day it reached the monastery. Other major works are *St. Peter Liberated by the Angel* by José de Ribera, and the set of works by Lucas Jordán including *Noah Inebriated by his Children* and *The Prayer in the Garden.*

The Altar of the Sacred Form

The most ambitious artistic project by the Madrid school of the last third of the XVII century was this altar, ordered to be built by Charles II and entrusted to José del Olmo, royal master builder, and Francisco Ricci, court painter. However, on August 2 1685 Francisco Ricci died in San Lorenzo, and his place was immediately taken by Claudio Coello. The first task undertaken by the new court painter was the completion of the painting begun by Ricci, the composition of which he had to change since it was not to the king's liking.

The work depicts the most significant moment in the ceremony held in the monastery on October 19 1684, when the prior, Francisco de los Santos, shows King Charles II the Sacred Form of Gorcum, in a sumptuous golden monstrance, before depositing it in the new tabernacle which was built for this purpose in the sacristy.

This relic entered San Lorenzo on November 7 1597, the day on which Philip II had persuaded its owners, the Marquis and Marchioness of Navarrés, to give it to the monastery. The new relic came from the German city of Gorcum, where a group of armed Protestants, called *zeeguezen* or beggars of the sea, had desecrated the church and crushed the Sacred Forms underfoot. To the astonishment of the troops, one of the Forms began to bleed after having been trampled by one of the soldiers' hobnail boot heels. News of this miraculous occurrence spread like wildfire all over Germany, transforming this new relic into an important instrument of Catholic propaganda. Having had a number of different owners, the Sacred Form was taken to Vienna by Ferdinand Weidmer, a captain in the army of the Emperor Rudolph II, and through his descendants it eventually came to Spain.

The reason why Charles II was forced to build this new altar was because Pope Innocent XI had demanded it of him as the condition by which the order of excommunication would be lifted from some of the nobles who formed the

king's government. This unpleasant situation had arisen because the Duke of Medina Sidonia and his followers had desecrated the temple when on January 17 1677 they came in search of Fernando Valenzuela, the royal favourite, who had hidden in the monastery.

The monarch took the offense as his own and decided to create a new homage to the Triumph of the Eucharist, taking the Sacred Form of Gorcum as its central element. The richness of the materials used (jasper, marble and gilt bronze) denotes the importance of the project, since with it Charles II left further evidence of the greatness of the House of Austria in San Lorenzo.

The Pantheons

The most spectacular moment of our visit occurs when, having descended the majestic staircase of the Royal Pantheon, we arrive in the middle of the funerary chamber and contemplate the urns which contain the mortal remains of one of the Earth's most powerful lineages. The creations of this room was the principal reason for Philip II's founding San Lorenzo; for this reason, Father Sigüenza says that "the creation of sepulchres for such illustrious heroes and princes being one of the prime motives for the foundation of this monastery, it would be a shortcoming to examine them only perfunctorily". We shall therefore follow his advice.

The arrival of the first royal corpses, those of Queen Isabelle of Valois and Prince Don Carlos, took place on June 6 1573, three years after the Hieronymite community had occupied the habitable part of the building. After they had been placed in the vault built below the altar of the Old Church, then called the *Iglesia del Prestado,* the king decided to take up the tombs of his parents and the rest of the Imperial Family and move them to the new monastery, although their final location was not yet ready.

Such a radical presence of death in the life of the monastery since its very beginnings is due to its nature of a work of expiation as the vehicle through which to attain the Grace of God. For XVI-century society death was the punishment for having committed original sin, the most direct consequences of which are the loss of saintliness and immortality. When the soul left the body, only God's help would make it possible for the individual to be saved, and this grace would be granted only on the basis of conduct during life on Earth. Life was thus a preparation for death, for the way people lived would determine their future life. The application of these ideas in San Lorenzo explains the tight relationship existing there between the divine order (basilica), the human order (palace) with death (pantheon) as the unifying element. Thanks to this complex structure, the building became the earthly model of what life would be like next to God, and the people living there privileged beings whose salvation was already assured.

After a number of different periods of trial and error, Philip II arranged the royal tombs beneath the main altar, creating three levels of reality. The first was the presbytery itself, where all public religious ceremonies were held; then came the funerary chamber, where the corpses were laid in cloth-lined wooden coffins, this place being conceived as an intermediate vault extending beneath the sacristy; finally, a circular funerary chapel communicating directly with the king's chambers, the monastery and the presbytery, for private worship. In this way the stipulations in the Emperor's will were satisfied as regards how his body should be placed: "The half of my body from the feet to the chest must be beneath the altar; the other half, from the chest to the head, must protrude. In this way, the priest saying mass will have to rest his feet on my chest and my head".

The present-day Royal Pantheon, however, in no way follows this plan, for when in 1621 Philip III stipulated how he was to be buried, reconstruction work on the piece had already begun. The formula used reads as follows: "(...) my body shall be carried with as little pomp as possible for burial in the Monastery of San Lorenzo el Real, which my Illustrious Father founded for his own burial and that of his successors

D. O. M.
LOCVS SACER MORTALITATIS EXVVIIS
CATHOLICORVM REGVM
A RESTAVRATORE VITAE CVIS ARAE MAXIMAE
AVSTRIACA ADHVC PIETATE SVBIACENT
OPTATAM DIEM EXPECTANTIVM.

QVAM POSTHVMAM SEDEM SIBI ET SVIS
CAROLVS CAESARVM MAX. INVOTIS HABVIT.
PHILIPPVS II REGVM PRVDENTIS. ELEGIT.
PHILIPPVS III. VERE PIVS INCHOAVIT.

PHILIPPVS IIII.
CLEMENTIA CONSTANTIA RELIGIONE MAGNVS
AVXIT ORNAVIT ABSOLVIT
AN. DOM. M.DC.LIIII.

who so wish". The king considered the great modesty and poverty of this chamber as being unworthy of his high dignity, and subsequent chronicles justify the new pantheon by saying that Philip II had built one chamber only as a deposit, expecting his successors to complete the project. Baroque society accepted the disillusionment of the world with deep pessimism which gave rise to the concept of life as a great theatre play whose final act is death. The monarchy occupied the summit of this scale of values, and the works of art they promoted should reflect their ideals of grandeur, authority and honour, since through these the rest of society could perceive the presence of God. The new Royal Pantheon is a faithful reflection of this concept, which justifies its architectural sumptuousness and richness of materials.

The Royal Pantheon

Construction began in 1617 under the direction of the architect Juan Gómez de Mora, who was responsible for its design. The project made use of the original funerary church, increasing it in size in order to endow it with better proportions and greater beauty. Work was interrupted in 1621, after the death of Philip III, and it was his successor, Philip IV, who in 1645 ordered the pantheon to be completed, entrusting the task to the architect Isidro Carbonell. The opening ceremony was finally held on March 16 1654.

To these names must be added those of Pedro de Lizgárate and Bartolomé Zumbigo, master builders who worked on the placing of the marble; Brother Nicolás de Madrid, a Hieronymite monk who found the solutions to the problems of drainage, ventilation and illumination; Juan Bautista Crescenzi, the Italian architect who was responsible for the decoration, and Diego Velázquez who, as palace *aposentador* (head steward) was required to give his opinion of the project.

Entrance to the mortuary chamber is by means of a wide staircase, lined with red marble and jasper and divided into

three sections. The descent begins at an elegant marble door with a two-leafed gilt bronze grille. Above there is a black marble plaque with a long Latin inscription listing the names of everyone involved with the work. The composition is crowned by the coat of arms of Philip IV flanked by two reclining feminine figures, the one with her head bowed representing faltering human nature, and the other symbolising hope. As we descend we pass four mahogany and ebony doors, the first two of which are false and are there to match the two in the second section and provide access to the former sacristy, now the deposit for mortal remains, and the former Prince's Pantheon.

Having passed through a second grille of gilt bronze we find ourselves in the Royal Pantheon itself. This impressive circular chamber, lined with marble and jasper and with gilt bronze adornments, is ten metres in diameter and almost eleven metres in height. It is divided into eight sides by paired pillars on whose entablement rests the dome, also divided into eight sections through which light enters from the *Patio de los Mascarones*. The altar, which stands opposite the entrance door, is presided over by a gilt bronze crucifix, the work of the Italian sculptor Doménico Guidi. This piece was commissioned as a replacement for the one by Gian Lorenzo Bernini, which was too big and did not fit. Bernini's work, transferred to the school chapel, was a gift from Pope Innocent X to Marian of Austria, Philip IV's second wife. The front of this altar was built in gilt bronze by the Hieronymite monks Eugenio de la Cruz and Juan de la Concepción, and in its centre appears *The Burial of Christ*. Other outstanding pieces here are the great gilt bronze chandelier made in Genoa by Virgilio Fenelli, and the wall lights in the form of angels by Clemente Censore from Milan.

Arranged around the chamber are the twenty-six elegant sepulchral grey marble urns, twelve on either side of the altar and two above the door, sustained by lion's claws and featuring a bronze plaque giving the name of the occupant. Following the established order, the kings on the left-hand side and the queen mothers of heirs to the throne on the right-hand side, we now go on an itinerary through the history of modern Spain in the company of its immediate protagonists.

We begin with Charles I of Spain and V of Germany (1500-1556), accompanied by his wife Isabel of Portugal (1503-1539). Both occupy the top biers on either side of the altar. Beneath them are Philip II (1527-1598) and his fourth wife, Anne of Austria (1549-1580). Next come Philip III (1578-1621) and Margaret of Austria (1584-1611). These two first sections are completed with Philip IV (1605-1665) and his first wife, Isabel of Bourbon (1603-1644), the mother of the Prince of Asturias, Baltasar Carlos, who died in 1646. The House of Austria ends with Charles II (1661-1700) and his mother Marian of Austria (1634-1696), the second wife of Philip IV, who occupy the first urns of the next sections.

After Charles II had died childless, the Spanish throne was occupied by Philip of Bourbon, Duke of Anjou, the great-grandson of Louis XIV of France. The new monarch, Philip V (1683-1743), who saw San Lorenzo as the symbol of the House of Habsburg, did not hesitate in ordering the burial here of the mortal remains of his first wife, Mar!a Luisa Gabriela of Savoy (1668-1714) and of his son, Luis I (1707-1724) who became king of Spain after his father's voluntary abdication. The first Bourbon monarch decided to be buried next to his second wife, Elisabeth Farnese (1692-1766) in the collegiate church of the Palace of San Ildefonso. Also missing from this pantheon is Ferdinand VI (1713-1759), Philip V's second son, who chose to be buried in the Monastery of La Visitación, also known as the Monastery of Las Salesas Reales, in Madrid, next to his wife Bárbara de Braganza (1711-1758).

After Ferdinand VI died childless, the crown fell to the king of Naples, Charles VII, third son of Philip V, who, having renounced his Italian kingdom, came to Spain as Charles III (1716-1788). With this sovereign the Monastery of San Lorenzo once again became the House of the King of Spain, and here we find his remains together with those of his wife, María Amalia of Saxony (1724-1760) and those of his successors Charles IV (1748-1819) and his wife María Luisa of Parma (1751-1819), with whom this section is completed.

We now proceed to the final two divisions where, following the same order, we find Ferdinand VII (1784-1833) next to his fourth wife, María Cristina of Naples (1806-1878); Isabella II (1830- 1904), who became queen thanks to the pragmatic sanction published by her father some months before her birth and who occupies the urn below that of her father. On the opposite side lies her husband, the king consort Francisco de Asís (1822-1902). Next come Alphonso XII (1857-1885) and his second wife, María Cristina de Austria (1858-1929). Queen María de la Mercedes (1860-1878), the first wife of this monarch is buried in the basilica (Chapel of St. Anne and St. John) waiting for her final resting place in the Cathedral of La Almudena in Madrid to be made ready.

We now reach the final urns in this section only one of which, as we see, is occupied: that on the kings' side, which contains the remains of Alphonso XIII (1886-1941), brought from Rome, where he died, to San Lorenzo in 1980. His wife, Victoria Eugenia de Battenberg (1887-1969), was brought from Lausanne in 1985 and deposited in the kings' mortal remains deposit, from whence she will be transferred in the urn opposite her husband's when protocol determines things thus.

As we can observe, the two urns over the door have still to be filled in order for the pantheon to be complete.

The Princes' Pantheon

Our itinerary now proceeds to the Princes' Pantheon, the most important XIX-century contribution to the Monastery of San Lorenzo. It became necessary because of the lack of space in the funerary chamber, which had been built for this purpose in the XVII century, and it was Isabella II

First room in the Panteón de Infantes

who commissioned the palace architect, José Segundo de Lema, to draw up and execute the plans. Work took place between 1862 and 1888, with a hiatus of ten years (1868-1877) due to political unrest.

The mausoleum consists of nine sepulchral chambers of different sizes situated beneath the sacristy, the prior's cell and part of the chapter rooms, taking advantage of the so-called *cantinas* or vaults which, according to Father Sigüenza, were "excellent pieces of great service for all the offices and ceremonies that took place in the great building." The whole complex is lined with white and grey marble from Carrara and Bardiglio and its most important decorative elements are the sculptures by Ponciano Ponzano, Jacopo Baratta and Giuseppe Galleotti. The style of these new dependencies derives from the low medieval Gothic of the XIV and XV centuries.

Having passed through the entrance grilles we find a grey marble plaque with an inscription in Latin explaining the purpose of the pantheon and naming the monarchs who ordered its construction. We then enter the first chamber, where the most interesting group of tombs is to be found. The first of these corresponds to Luisa Carlota de Borbón, wife of Francisco de Paula, the brother of Ferdinand VII. This tomb was originally in the Chapel of the Virgins, from whence it was transferred when the pantheon was opened. The architectural part in white Carrara marble is the work of Domingo Gómez de la Puente, while the gilt bronze statue of the Princess in attitude of prayer is by Ponzano. Lastly, worthy of mention is the tomb of the Duke and Duchess of Montpensier, together with two of their daughters, Cristina and Amalia, upon whose sepulchres is a reclining statue, one of which is signed by Aimé Millet, Paris, 1880, and that of María Josefa de Borbón, the sister of Charles IV, against the wall. The chamber is presided over by an altar with a painting by Carlo Veronese depicting *The Descent from the Cross,* framed in marble and porphyry.

After passing through an empty chamber we reach the tomb of María Teresa de Borbón, the sister of Alphonso XIII, designed by the architect Landecho and built from dark marble with gilt bronze lamps. This sepulchre was intended to be occupied by two people, although now only the Infanta of Spain rests inside since her husband decided to be buried alongside his second wife.

The next funerary chamber, almost empty, served as the resting place for part of the family of Isabella II. As we see, each of the tombs is decorated with the name of the royal personage occupying it, an epitaph written in Latin and the corresponding coat of arms.

In the last chamber on this side we find the grave of John of Austria, bastard son of the Emperor and victor at the Battle of Lepanto. Upon the bed appears the recumbent statue of the hero dressed in armour and holding the copy of a sword, the original of which is preserved in the Royal Armoury. The work, a prodigy of realist detail, was modelled by Ponciano and executed by Galeotti in Carrara marble.

We now proceed into the children's mausoleum, in the

centre of which is the polygonal, white marble tomb which, by virtue of its decoration, is popularly known as *la tarta* (the cake). The altar is presided over by the famous canvas by Lavinia Fontana, a copy of Raphael's *Madonna of Loreto,* which depicts the Holy Family with St. John the Child, watching over the sleeping Christ.

The three following chambers are flanked by heralds, bearing axes, made from white Carrara marble by Ponzano. The last one contains the mortal remains of the members of the House of Austria buried here.

Appendix

List of all the royal personages who rest in the pantheon:

House of Austria

1.- Imperial Family

In the Royal Pantheon lie the Emperor Charles and his wife, Isabella of Portugal, together with his sisters Eleonor of France and María of Hungary, and his children, the Infantes Ferdinand, John and María, together with John of Austria.

2.- Family of Philip II

This monarch rests in the Royal Pantheon together with his fourth wife, Anne of Austria. In the Princes' Pantheon lie Princess María of Portugal, his first wife, together with her son, Prince Charles. His second wife, Mary Tudor, is missing, since she is buried in Westminster Abbey. Then come Isabelle of Valois, his third wife, and the Infantes Carlos Lorenzo and María, in the children's pantheon, and Princes Ferdinand and Diego, all children of Anne of Austria. Finally we must mention the Archduke Wenceslas of

View of the last three rooms of the Pantheon.

Austria, the son of María, the king's sister, and the princes of Savoy, Felipe Manuel and Manuel Filiberto, the sons of Catalina Micaela, the daughter of Philip II, together with Ferdinand of Savoy, son of Manuel Filiberto.

3.- Family of Philip III

Philip III and his wife Margaret of Austria rest in the Royal Pantheon together with their children Alonso Mauricio and María, in the children's mausoleum, and Margarita Francisca, Carlos and the Cardinal-Infante Fernando, Governor of the Netherlands, buried in the Princes' Pantheon. With them also is the Archduke Charles of Austria, son of María of Hungary, the king's sister.

4.- Family of Philip IV

The king lies in the Royal Pantheon beside his two wives, Isabella of Bourbon and Marian of Austria. Also buried here are the children of his first marriage, Prince Baltasar Carlos, María Margarita, Margarita María Catalina, Margarita María, Isabel María Teresa and María Ana Antonia. From his second marriage are the children Felipe Próspero, Fernando and María Concepción Ambrosia. Also buried here are his bastard sons Francisco Fernando and Juan José of Austria.

5.- Family of Charles II

The last member of the dynasty rests in the Royal Pantheon, while his two wives, Marie Louise of Orleans and Marianne of Neoburg are buried in the Princes' Pantheon.

House of Bourbon

1.- Family of Philip V

Although the monarch himself does not rest in this pantheon, his first wife, María Luisa of Savoy and his first son, Luis I, lie in the Royal Pantheon. In the children's pantheon lie Felipe Luis and Felipe Pedro, the offspring of his first marriage, and Francisco, of his second. By request of the king, also buried here is the Duke of Vendome, José Luis de Borbón, the bastard son of Louis XIV, who died in Valencia during the War of Succession.

In 1800 Charles IV ordered the remains of the Infante Luis Antonio, son of Philip IV and Elisabeth Farnese, to be brought to this pantheon, they originally having lain in the Chapel of San Pedro de Alcántara in Arenas (Avila).

2.- Family of Charles III

The king lies beside his wife, María Amalia of Saxony in the Royal Pantheon, while his children Francisco Javier, Antonio Pascual, María Josefa and Gabriel lie in that of the Princes. Gabriel lies next to his wife, María Ana of Portugal, and his two children Carlos José and María Carlota.

3.- Family of Charles IV

On September 18 1819 the corpses of Charles IV and his wife, María Luisa de Parma, arrived from Italy to be placed in the Royal Pantheon. Already resting here were his children Carlos Clemente, Carlos Eusebio, Felipe, Fernando Carlos, Felipe María Francisco, María Luisa and María Teresa, who now lie in the children's mausoleum. Other children of this matrimony lying in the pantheon are: Francisco de Paula together with his wife, Luisa Carlota of Naples, and their children Francisco, Eduardo, Luisa, Cristina and María Teresa Carolina (the latter in the children's pantheon); María Luisa and her husband, Luis de Borbón, king of Etruria; and María Amalia.

4.- Family of Ferdinand VII

This monarch is in the Royal Pantheon together with his fourth wife, María Cristina of Naples, while his first three spouses, María Antonia of Naples, Isabel de Braganza and María Josefa Amalia of Saxony lie in the Princes' Pantheon. Together with them are the little girl María Isabel Luisa, daughter of Isabel of Braganza, and María Luisa, daughter of María Cristina of Naples, who rests beside her husband, Antonio de Orleans, Duke of Montpensier, and their children, María Cristina, María Amalia, Felipe and María.

5.- Family of Isabella II

Isabella II lies next to her husband, Francisco de Asís, in the Royal Pantheon, while in the children's pantheon rest Margarita, who was stillborn, Francisco Leopoldo, María Cristina, María de la Concepción, María del Pilar and Eulalia (in the mortal remains deposit) together with her husband, Antonio de Orleans. Missing is the Infanta Isabel, known affectionately as *La Chata*, who is buried in the Collegiate Church of the Palace of San Ildefonso, although the Count of Girgenti, her husband, lies in this pantheon. Together with them is Sebastián Gabriel de Borbón who, although he died in exile through having embraced the Carlist cause, is buried here as Infante of Spain thanks to the right granted by Charles III to his son Gabriel, according to which all the latter's successors would enjoy this privilege.

6.- Family of Alphonso XII

Alphonso XII lies next to his second wife, María Cristina of Austria, in the Royal Pantheon. In that of the princes lie their daughters, Princess María de las Mercedes accompanied by her children Alphonso and Isabel Alfonsa (in the mortal remains deposit), and the Infanta María Teresa, together with her children Luis Alfonso (in the mortal remains deposit) and María de las Mercedes.

7.- Family of Alphonso XIII

Alphonso XIII has been since 1980 in the Royal Pantheon, while his wife, Victoria Eugenia, is in the mortal remains deposit. In the Princes' Pantheon are Prince Alphonso and the Infantes Gonzalo and Jaime (this latter in the princes mortal remains deposit) and in the one for children a stillborn baby.

The Platerías

As a communication area between the pantheons and the chapter rooms, a wide passage known as the *platerías* (silversmiths') is used which corresponds to the *cantinas* or vaults which run beneath the floor level of the monastery, part of which was used to house the Infantes' Pantheon. The name derives from the fact that the San Lorenzo silversmith workshops were originally located here. This architectural space was recovered and opened to the public on the occasion of the IV Centenary of the completion of the works of San Lorenzo. At the moment these rooms are empty of decoration, so that the architecture itself is the true protagonist. Its three rooms constitute one of the few samples of the constructional perfection and refined style achieved by Juan Bautista de Toledo, the first architect to work on the building.

The Clausura

Although closed to visitors, worthy of mention is the area occupied by the Augustinian community, known as the *clausura* (inner recess or sanctuary), since access to it is limited by the normal demands of religious life.

Most of the monks' cells are around the Main High Cloister. Outstanding among these are the Prior's High Cell, now a reading room, and the Bishop's Cell, reserved for illustrious visitors to the monastery. The remaining depend-

General view of the Aula Magna,
former lay dormitory.

Balsa de Necesarias

encies that open onto the cloister are: the lay dormitory, now the assembly hall; the Choir Sacristy or Hall of Capes, so called because here the capes were kept for the singers in the festivities (today it is used as a chapel); the Morals Classroom, the place where the monks gathered to study and discuss matters relating to this doctrine; and St. Theresa's Chamber, since it was here that the saint's writings, now in the Library, were originally kept.

We now proceed to the four smaller cloisters, designed by Juan Bautista de Toledo, among which are distributed the remainder of the parts that form the monastery. the most interesting areas here are the Refectory, which has been preserved almost without any major modification; the *balsa de necesarias,* one of the few examples of XVI-century services architecture; the *ropería* (clothing room), now the library's manuscript room; and the *Lucerna* or hollow interior tower, which provides the corridors with light.

5 - THE LIBRARY

In the Foundation Charter of the Monastery of San Lorenzo it is stipulated that a library shall be created, designed to be the first public establishment of this kind in Spain. This royal decision was in response to the important issue raised by a group of Spanish intellectuals and humanists, who spoke of the need to gather together in one building, as was being done in Rome and Florence, all the most important manuscripts and publications which at the time were scattered among a great number of monasteries and private libraries. One of the figures who most influenced this resolution was the Spanish scholar Juan Páez de Castro (1512-1570), who shortly after Philip II had occupied the throne sent the monarch a *Memorial sobre los libros y utilidad de la librería y orden y traza que en ella se ha de tener*, in which he explained the need to the new king and informed him of the prestige such an act would bring.

Among the places considered to house this ambitious project were the university cities of Salamanca and Alcalá de Henares, but the king's will on this point was unshakable: the new library would form an integral part of the new monastery.

Philip II sought the advice of a number of Spanish humanists as to the criteria to follow when it came to collecting and preserving this bibliographical heritage. Prominent among the opinions expressed was that of the historian from Córdoba Ambrosio de Morales (1513-1591), who proposed the creation of a library specialising in the acquisition and custody of manuscripts, by virtue of their character as unique and original works, alongside the great number and variety of printed books, which would thus mean that the new library would surpass in importance others such as the Marcian in Venice, the Medicea Laurenciana in Florence or the Vatican in Rome. In his memorial, titled *Parecer sobre la librería para El Escorial*, the Cordobese sage made interesting observations as to how the books should be guarded to prevent their being stolen, and even proposed a system of chains so that single pages

*General view of the Library with the
former exhibition of books.*

could not be removed. This same opinion was also expressed by the humanist Benito Arias Montano (1527-1598), who moreover suggested that two parallel libraries should be created, one for public use and the other restricted, where the original manuscripts would be kept.

The king himself was the first to endow the new establishment with his own personal library, consisting of over one thousand two hundred volumes, between manuscripts and printed books. His initiative was followed by many other leading figures of the time, whose names tell of the cultural importance and quality of the books. Outstanding among the donations were the private libraries of Philip II's secretary, the politician and scholar González Pérez (1506-1566), of Juan Páez de Castro and Benito Arias Montano, and of the noblemen Diego Hurtado de Mendoza (1503-1575) and Juan de Borja (1475-1497), second Duke of Gandía. Complete libraries from other royal foundations were also donated, such as those of the Monastery of Guadalupe and the Royal Chapel of Granada. Furthermore, innumerable purchases were made all over Europe, in which neither effort nor money were spared. In the mid XVII century the libraries of the Mûlây of Morocco and of Philip IV's favourite, the Count-Duke of Olivares (1587-1645), were acquired for El Escorial.

In an attempt to keep the Royal Library up-to-date as far as publications were concerned, on January 12 1619 Philip II issued his famous decree obliging all booksellers and printers to reserve for the library a copy of every work published in all the Kingdoms of Spain, a resolution which was not however kept with all the zeal the monarch would have desired.

Outstanding among the unfortunate occurrences that have depleted the number of volumes kept here was the voracious fire of 1671, which consumed over four thousand manuscripts.

Today the Royal Library contains some forty-five thousand volumes, mostly from the XV and XVI centuries, and a collection of over five thousand manuscripts arranged in order of numerical importance in the following languages: Arabic,

Latin, Spanish, Greek, Italian, Hebrew, Catalan, French, Chinese, Persian, Portuguese, Turkish, Armenian, German and Nahuatl.

Philip II's plans went beyond the creation of a library that would contain books and manuscripts only. His vision of knowledge was universal and many-sided, so that in addition to books he also collected terrestrial and celestial globes, maps, and mathematical and scientific instruments, as well as a set of portraits of pontiffs, emperors, kings and eminent scholars. Unfortunately, however, little of this remains, as we shall shortly see.

The Print Room

Within the complex organisation of the building, the Library is in a strategic position, between the college and the monastery, as the common place for both monks and students, and opposite the House of God, thus creating a counterpoint between human and divine wisdom. The first provisional site for the library was the novices' dormitory, now the assembly hall, where a total of ten thousand volumes were gathered to be arranged by Father Juan de San Jerónimo, the first librarian, assisted by Arias Montano, who was summoned by Philip II in 1577 to carry out this task. The first classification was done according to languages and subjects, after the manuscripts had been separated from the printed books. However, the definitive cataloguing was not completed until 1593, the year in which the decoration of the main library hall was finished. The new order was the brainchild of Father Sigüenza, the second librarian, who decided to keep the printed books in the main hall, the manuscripts in the adjoining ones and the upper chamber for the books least consulted.

Today only the main or print room can be visited, situated above the main access vestibule to the *Patio de Reyes*. This room, "the largest and noblest of all"according to Father Sigüenza, is fifty-four metres long by nine wide and ten high,

The Library ceiling,
by Tibaldi and his studio.

and is covered by an elegant semi-cylindrical vault oriented north-south and divided into seven sections. The paintings here respond to the universalist ideal with which Philip II wanted to endow the building, and were produced by the Italian artist Pellegrino Tibaldi and his studio who, following the directions of Juan de Herrera, depicted on this vault all the knowledge of the time, symbolised by the Seven Liberal Arts or Sciences imparted in the universities, together with Philosophy and Theology and the principle of all renaissance culture. The iconographical programme, the most ambitious in the whole monastery, was devised by Benito Arias Montano. Each art is represented by a matron surrounded by children bearing its corresponding symbols. Beneath, serving as bases for the lunettes, we find four ages or artists who were outstanding in their respective disciplines. Finally, the frieze stretching from the cornice to the shelves and attributed to Bartolomé Carduccho depicts stories illustrating famous events related to knowledge. Worthy of mention here are the "grotto" style ornamental fringes by the Genoese artists Nicolás Granello and Fabrizio Castello.

Description

Top Part: Mural Painting

Philosophy

Coinciding with the frontispiece of the end wall, where the entrance to the room stands, we first of all come across *Philosophy,* considered to be the mother of all human science and knowledge. It is depicted as a young matron seated before a globe, symbolising her universal character and unlimited power. She is accompanied by Aristotle, Plato, Seneca and Socrates, the most important philosophers of Classical Antiquity.

On the frieze the subject of *The School of Athens* appears, showing its two most important trends: the Stoics led by

Zenon, who based their principles on strict, austere morals, and the Academics, whose highest ideal is summarised in the phrase "know yourself".

Grammar

The vault begins with the Trivium, or the three liberal arts related to eloquence: Grammar, Rhetoric and Dialectics. The first of the three liberal arts appears as a large matron seated on clouds and surrounded by children carrying primers and other books. She holds in her hands a laurel wreath and disciplines as symbols of reward and punishment, these being the basis of the renaissance educational system.

On either side, beneath the lunettes with figures of *ignutis*, or naked youths, are four celebrated grammarians: on the right Marcus Terencius Varon and Sextus Pomponius, and on the left, Tiberius Donatus and Antonio de Nebrija.

On the friezes we read *The Construction of the Tower of Babel*, as the moment of the birth of Grammar from the confusion of languages, beside its mythical creator, Nemrod; and *The School of Grammar of Babylon*, founded by Nebuchadnezzar in order to teach Chaldaic to Hebrew children, among whom we see four adolescents: Ananias, Azarias, Michael and Daniel who, feeding only on water and vegetables had the clearest minds in the whole of babylon.

In the space between the columns and beneath templets appear two great Roman historians: Pliny the Elder and Titus Livius.

Rhetoric

The art of eloquence is represented by an elegantly dressed matron who holds in one of her hands Mercury's wand, symbol of pagan eloquence. On one side we see a somewhat disproportioned lion which, according to Father Sigüenza, means that "the power of good speech tames even the most ferocious of beasts".

*"The Building of The Tower of Babel",
attributed to Carducho.*

In the lunettes we find, on the right, two great Greek orators: Isocrates and Demosthenes, and opposite them, creating a clear parallel, two Roman rhetoricians: Cicero and Quintillian.

The friezes contain scenes relative to the power of the word. On the one hand we have *Cicero Defending Cayus Rabirius before the Senate*. Opposite we see the representation of the *Gallic Hercules with Chains of Gold and Silver Emerging from his Mouth*. The scene follows a text by Lucian which tells how Hercules, the God of Eloquence for the Gauls, moved multitudes by virtue of the force of his eloquence, symbolised by the chains.

The protruding arch is used to depict four major poets from Classical Antiquity: Homer and Pindar from the Greek tradition, and Virgil and Horace from the Latin world.

Dialectics

The art of dialogue and discussion is personified in a woman with arms outstretched. Her right hand is open, symbolising the ability to expound a hypothesis, while the left one is closed, representing the skill of summarising this same supposition in a concise way. Her head bears two horns, or one half moon, representing the dilemma or argument that stems

PLINIO

from two opposing suppositions in order to reach the same conclusion.

In the lunettes we find four Greek philosophers: Zenon of Elea and Meliso on the right; and Protagoras and Origenes on the left.

The episodes chosen for the frieze are *Zenon of Elea Showing his Disciples the Gates of Truth and Lies,* and opposite this *St. Ambrose and St. Augustine Arguing, before the Latter's Conversion,* together with a kneeling St. Monica who pleads with God to save her son. Beneath we read *A logica Augustini, libera nos, Domine* (Free us, Oh Lord, from Augustinian logic), a litany which St. Ambrose would repeat every time he argued with his nephew about matters of Faith.

Arithmetic

The remaining Liberal Arts were grouped under the epigraph of Quadrivium, or sciences related to mathematics, study of which began after the Trivium had been mastered.

Our description continues with arithmetic which, like the foregoing disciplines, is symbolised by a matron surrounded by children before whom she is calculating a problem, using the fingers of her hand.

Representing this science on our right are Arquitas of Tarento and Boecius, and on our left Jordan of Saxony and Jenocrates of Calcedonia.

The scenes that appear in the frieze are *Solomon and the Queen of Sheba*, in which we see how the wise king of Israel solves all the arithmetical problems and puzzles posed by the queen. The table of numbers, the scales and a measuring rod, together with the phrase *Everything is made with numbers, weights and measures* (which appears written in Hebrew on the fold of the cloth) symbolise the Book of Wisdom, presumably written by Solomon himself. On the opposite side we see *The Gymnosophists or Indian Sages Mathematically Discussing the Qualities of the Soul.*

Music

Music was also considered part of mathematics since, as the Greek philosopher Pythagoras showed, numbers are the basis of sounds. It is here represented in the form of a beautiful woman playing a seven-stringed lute, a figure reminiscent of Euterpe, the muse of music, who is normally depicting strumming this instrument. Next to her is a group of children with instruments and musical scores and a large singing swan, the animal of Apollo, God of music.

Accompanying this art are Pythagoras and Tubalcain opposite Anphion and Orpheus.

Beneath these figures we see the stories of *David Playing his Harp to Placate the Rage of King Saul.* In this way, thanks to music, Saul is able to liberate his evil spirits, who leave his mouth in the form of demons. Opposite we have *Orpheus and Eurydice*, representing the moment when Orpheus, having put the hound Cancerber, guardian of Hades, to sleep with the sound of his lyre, prepares to liberate his loved one Eurydice, who walks behind him.

Beneath elegant templets, in the next plaster border arch, we encounter the gods Mercury and Apollo on our right, and Pan and Miseno on our left.

Geometry

The most noble of the mathematical disciplines is represented by a circumspect and inward-looking matron, surrounded by children playing with mathematical instruments, taking measurements with a compass.

She is accompanied in the lunettes by Archimedes and Juan of Monterregio on the right, and by Aristarch of Samos and Abdelaziz Alcabicio on the left.

The scenes chosen for the frieze are *The Egyptian Priests Dividing the Fields,* an operation they had to carry out every time the River Nile recovered its normal course in order thus to mark the boundaries of each property, and *Archimedes Slain by the Romans* since, being absorbed in the solution of a prob-

"Geometry", one of the liberal arts, making calculations with a compass, his symbol.

lem of geometry, the Greek sage did not notice the presence of the Roman soldiers who, after the surrender of the city of Syracuse, took his life.

On the decorative border, beneath a templet, we find Dicearco Sículo opposite Eratostenes Cirengo.

Astrology

The last discipline of the Quadrivium is represented by a large matron seated on a globe and holding a celestial sphere in her arms. In her right hand she holds a compass, alluding to geometry, the science she uses with which to cary out her calculations of the movement of the stars. She is accompanied by children bearing other precision instruments.

In the niches we have, on the right, Alphonso X the Wise and Ptolemy and, on the left, Euclides and Juan Sacrobosco.

In the freizes beneath the lunettes we encounter *Dionisio*

Areopagita and Apollophanes Observing the Eclipse of the Sun on the Day of the Death of Christ since, according to tradition, when these Greek sages saw this phenomenon from Athens, Areopagita exclaimed "Either the God of Nature is suffering or the machine of the world is disintegrating!" On the opposite side we see *The Sick King Hezekia is Visited by the Prophet Isiah*, announcing that the Lord concedes him fifteen years more of life and, as proof of this, we see a solar quadrant whose shadow miraculously recedes.

Theology

The iconographical programme concludes with Theology, since this is the supreme science of the Revelation; it is represented by a young, graceful woman, who admits neither corruption nor old age, beneath a temple symbolising the Church, where she has her throne and professorial chair. Over her head, sustained by a shining halo, there is a crown, symbol of her superiority and royalty. In her hands she holds the Bible, showing the Four Doctors of the Latin Church: St. Jerome, St. Ambrose, St. Gregory Magno and St. Augustin.

The frieze depicts *The Council of Nicea*, held in that Greek city in 325. During this Ecumenical Council, presided over by the papal legate, Osio de Córdoba and with the Emperor Constantine among those attending, the doctrine of Arius, which denies the consubstantiality of the Father and the Son, was condemned (the moment represented here) and the prayer of the Credo was fixed as the Christians' profession of faith.

Side Walls: Shelves, Painting, Sculpture

On the side walls and all around the room are the splendid shelves with which the "prudent king" endowed the Library to house the collection of books. They were designed by Juan de Herrera and made by the Italian Giuseppe Flecha, assisted by the Spaniards Gamboa and Serrano, following a sober decorative line based on the beauty of the Tuscan order. The different woods used (mahogany, cedar, ebony, orange wood, walnut and terebinth) bestow upon the group elegant tonal nuances which match the rest of the decoration in the room.

There are fifty-four sets of six shelves each, which throughout the XVIII century were protected by doors with wire mesh, except for the second one, which was closed inside a wooden door with a lock. All the shelves rest on marble and jasper socles.

The books were placed with their backs facing outwards. Their titles were thus visible and they were not only easier to handle but suffered less wear and tear when taken out. Being furthermore bound in calf's hide and gilt, they created a greater effect of sumptuousness.

On each of the four pillars was placed a full-length portrait of one of the kings of the House of Austria. In chronological order, these are:

- The Emperor Charles V at the age of forty-nine, in the armour he wore at the battle of Mühlberg. The painting, the copy of an original, now lost, by Titian, is signed and dated by Juan Pantoja de la Cruz (1606).

- King Philip II, also by Pantoja de la Cruz, at the age of seventy-one and dressed in black.

- King Philip III, by the same *madrileño* painter, dressed in armour at the age of twenty-three. The work is signed and dated (1609).

- King Charles II, last in the line of the House of Austria, at the age of fourteen and in full formal dress, the work of Juan Carreño de Miranda. This pillar was originally occupied by Velázquez's famous brown and silver portrait of Philip IV, which was stolen during the Napoleonic invasion and is now the property of the National Gallery, London.

In the window recesses are portraits of Benito Arias Montano and Francisco Pérez Bayer, both by an unknown artist, and of Father José de Sigüenza, attributed to Vicente Carducho.

The only pieces of sculpture are a gypsum bust of the Spanish seaman Jorge Juan, and a marble bust, brought

"Monetario" of the Library

from Herculaneum by Charles III, which might be a portrait
of Cicero. Finally, there are two stucco medallions which
reproduce both sides of the medal by Jacome Trezzo which
Philip II presented as a gift to Juan de Herrera.

Furniture

Along the length of the room there are eight tables of different provenance. Immediately after entering we come
across a rich, fine wood marquetry table top from the XVII
century. Then follow five rectangular tables in grey marble
with bronze borders, made during the reign of Philip II,
used to keep books below, and above to exhibit some of the
scientific instruments acquired for the Library. Placed between these are two smaller single-pedestal tables in porphyry, the work of Bartolomé Zumbigo and ordered to be
placed here by Philip IV. At the other end of the room is an
interesting pine wood armillary sphere, in the Ptolemaic
system which placed the Earth in the centre of the

Universe, made by Antonio Santucci in Florence in 1582 for Cardinal Claudio Le Baume.

Worthy of mention also is the exquisite piece in fine woods standing beneath the portrait of Father Sigüenza, made during the mid XVIII century to house the coin collection. It stands on a XVI-century table which, so tradition has it, was the one used by Sigüenza himself.

Exit is by means of the library cloister, through a rich XVIII- century marquetry door. Over the lintel there is a false black tablet warning that "anyone who dares remove books or objects from this library will be excommunicated". The cloister is decorated with paintings, outstanding among which is the collection of portraits by the Spanish painter and scholar Antonio Ponz.

6.- PALACES

We now consider the non religious or erudite dependencies of the Monastery of San Lorenzo, known as the palaces. These were created around the *Patio del Palacio* and the rear part of the basilica, in an arrangement similar to the one we saw in the main cloister of the monastery. The need for space meant that this fine cloister was divided into three smaller ones, the largest of which is today known as the Royal or Coach Patio, and the smaller ones the Patio of *Patinejos de Boca* and of *Oficios* or *de la Cava*, the initial balance thus being altered.

Access to the dependencies of the National Heritage is through the central door on the northern façade, the same entrance used by his majesty's *"personal de boca"* (literally: mouth staff), who prepared the meals for the king and the royal family. On the lintel of the main door of the entrance hall is the tablet marking the beginning of the royal kitchen. This room and others now ceded to the college were occupied by the members of this staff. In the main room, the present-day cafeteria, was the great fire, as can clearly be seen from the outside by the situation of the large chimney with four draughts.

The Palacio de los Austrias (Palace of the House of Austria)

Standing inside the galleries of the *Patio Real* (Royal Patio) we can attempt mentally to reconstruct this palace. The dependencies to the north were originally, and in this order, the dining room of the Knights of the Court, the hall in which members of the royal family got down from their carriages and the ambassadors' quarters. Next came the main staircase, occupying the same space as the one which today leads up to the offices of the Delegation of the National Heritage and, at the base of the *Torre de Damas*, the *balsa de necesarias* or toilet cisterns. On the eastern side were the reception rooms for the

royal quarters, outstanding among which is the main hall or *Salón de Honor,* where El Greco's *Martyrdom of St. Mauricius* now hangs. Although the use and layout of these dependencies were altered during the XVIII century, the architectural configuration of the gallery of this patio has never been changed, and it is still possible today to appreciate the great beauty of this area with its delicate interplay between walls and openings. The northern and eastern sides are decorated with Flemish canvases, painted early in the XVII century, representing battles during the Flanders campaign, namely *The Blockade of Paris*, *The Battle of the Dunes of Newport*, *The Taking of Maestricht* and *The Siege of Calais*. On the south wall hang Luca Cambiaso's six enormous canvases, ordered by Philip II, which depict the Battle of Lepanto. The paintings were originally in the promenade gallery of the summer palace until, due to their poor state, they were moved to the basement. They were rescued from here in 1856 and, having been restored, hung in this gallery. The episodes represented are: *Departure from the Port of Messina of the Allied Fleet under Don John of Austria*, *The Christian Armada Engages that of the Turks*, *Both Armadas in Battle Formation at the Start of the Combat*, *The Act of Boarding*, *Removal of the Remains of the Turkish Fleet under Cover of Twilight* and *Return of the Victorious Fleet to the Port of Messina*.

On the first floor and in the loft of this palace were placed the quarters of all the court staff who accompanied the king to San Lorenzo. The rooms were on the western, northern and eastern sides only of the Royal Patio, looking outwards, since the southern end was occupied by the basilica. The knights and their servants were accommodated on the western and eastern sides, while the princes, infantes and other members of the royal family lived on the eastern side. The top gallery was divided into two large rooms also integrated into palace life, constituting what today is referred to as the *galería de paseo* (promenade gallery). With the arrival of the Bourbon court, in the XVIII century, this floor was also thoroughly rearranged, and only the Royal Gallery, today called the *Sala de Batallas* (Hall of Battles) was respected.

"Batlle of La Higueruela". Detail.

The monarchs' private quarters were built around the presbytery of the basilica, around the *Patio de Mascarones* (Patio of Masks), this being the area which is today called the *Palacio de los Austrias* and which in fact are the *Cuartos Reales* (monarchs' quarters).

Our itinerary begins at the two doors situated at the end of the eastern gallery, which provide access to the *Cuartos Reales* and to a staircase that links all the floors from the vaults to the lofts. Climbing this staircase we reach

The Sala de Batallas

T he impressive Hall of Battles has been known thus since the XVIII century when, after Charles III had rearranged the Royal Quarters, it lost its prominence within palace etiquette. Its original name was the *Galería Real* or Royal Gallery, although in some descriptions it figures as the "main", "long" and even "large" gallery. These adjectives denote its importance in the world of the XVI century and, for the same reason, justify its careful decoration. This kind of room was widely used during the Renaissance, since it provided the interior of palaces with large covered areas where it was possible to pass the time strolling or attending theatre performances or concerts. It was rarely used as a ballroom, since it was considered too cramped for such a purpose. On occasions it was also used as the venue for royal audiences.

Its situation can be considered strategic, since it is directly linked not only to the monarchs' quarters, but also to those of the remainder of the royal family, the basilica and the college. Its use was restricted to the king and the paintings that decorate it were conceived according to an iconographical and politico-religious programme which justified the sovereign's warlike acts before God and he himself. The Hispanic Monarchy had accepted the sacred mission of keeping faith united in the Catholic Church against attacks by both Turks and Protestants. Such a major undertaking, which enjoyed God's direct protection, transformed Spain and Philip II into the true protectors of the new order that had arisen as a result of the Council of Trent. Warlike iconography here therefore acquired a religious significance, becoming one of the clearest attestations of divine protection of the earthly plans of the Prudent King.

The authors of this major project were Fabrizio Castello, Nicolás Granello, Lázaro Tavarón and Orazio Cambiasso, artists who had come to the monastery in the company of Luca Cambiasso. It is estimated that they began work in 1585 and that, after many interruptions, considered their task finished in 1589.

The decoration is conceived in such a way that in order to understand it we have to walk all the way around the room. We begin at the main wall, where *The Battle of La Higuerela* is related, in which John II of Castile defeated the Granada Moors of Sierra Elvira in 1431. This event, which in reality was nothing more than a minor skirmish, was nevertheless used as evidence of God's support of the Christian monarchs. The choice of this episode is justified by Father Sigüenza, who explains that Philip II ordered it copied from a serge tapestry of the same theme which had been found in the Alcázar of Segovia. The description of the feat is exhaustive, as if it were the illustration to a book, and the main protagonists are the fine figures of John II and his favourite, Don Alvaro de Luna. It culminates in the terrible confrontation that led to the taking of the city and the slaughter of the civilian population, an act thoroughly alien to the Spanish medieval spirit.

We now reach the first end wall, which describes the *Chastisement of the Isle of Tercera* by the Spanish Armada.

We continue with scenes hanging between the windows, which narrate nine episodes of Philip II's French campaign, whose culminating moment was August 10 1557 with the taking of St. Quentin. The events described are: *Preparations for the Siege,* with the arrival of the king's fearsome Black Guard, *The Beginning of the Siege of St. Quentin, The Taking of St. Quentin, The Spanish Troops Advance on the Castle of Hayn, The Siege of the Castle of Hayn, The Taking of Chatelet, The Siege of the City of Gravellines, The Taking of Gravellines* and *The Encampment of*

*The French campaign: "Preparations
for the Siege of St. Quentin".*

146

the King of Spain between the Towns of Amiens and Doullens. This campaign ended with the signing of the Treaty of Château-Cambrésis, by which King Henri II of France accepted the Catholic faith.

On the other end wall we see an episode from *The Conquest of the Isle of Tercera.*

Outstanding in this room is the exquisite "grotto" style ceiling decoration, the work of the same team of Italian artists.

The Cuartos Reales

T he name *Cuartos Reales* or Royal Quarters refers to the set of rooms the monarchs occupied every time they came to San Lorenzo. Access to them was provided from the Royal Patio or from the Royal Gallery (*Sala de Batallas),* and a number of different routes allowed the visitor (depending on his importance or degree of familiarity with the monarch) to reach either the audience room or even the royal bed chamber.

Our itinerary begins at the patio gallery, and we enter this time through the last door on the eastern side. The corridor that runs around the Chapel of St. Anne in the basilica leads us to the first room, known today as the *Sala de los Morteros* (Hall of Mortars) by virtue of the excellent examples of this weapon, dating from the XVII century, displayed on the tables. The walls are decorated with Spanish paintings, also from the XVII century: *The Banishment of Agar* and *Elias and the Angel* by Juan Antonio de Frías y Escalante, and *Visit to the Monastery of San Lorenzo* and *Visit to El Campillo* (the country house which the monks from the monastery used for relaxation), by Benito Manuel de Agüero.

We would originally have now found the main staircase that linked the three levels of this part of the building; however, subsequent alterations have converted it into the flight we now climb.

The rooms we are about to visit were restored early this century, thanks to the archaeological work carried out by José

María Florit, curator of the Royal Armoury. Although the decoration of these rooms is not the original one, what we see today introduces us fully to the austere environment that characterised them at the end of the XVI century. This reconstruction is perfectly valid if we bear in mind that the furniture decoration of the Royal Sites was an element that varied with considerable frequency, since members of the royal family, when they travelled from one residence to another, normally did so taking with them their favourite works of art, with which they redecorated their rooms. The objects contained here belong mostly to the period of the reign of Philip II and those of his immediate successors, since it was they who deposited them in San Lorenzo. The true task consisted in grouping them in these rooms in order to display them in the environments for which they were originally intended.

Critics of the Philippine monarchy, who gave rise to the *leyenda negra* or black legend, saw in this monastery Philip II's secret "haunt", imagining a dark, labyrinthine building suitable more for a "predator" than for a renaissance prince. However, if we take the time to visit this monastery properly, we gradually discover the profound, rich personality of this man whose desire it was to gather in San Lorenzo humanity's greatest creations in praise of the Lord. Its rooms continue to echo this ideal, and for this reason they are spacious and bathed in light. Their interiors are charged with a sober, far from ostentatious richness, reflecting the personality of a cultured, balanced monarch who controlled the destiny of the world for over twenty years. Clear evidence of this are details such as the Talavera tile socles and the clay tile flooring. In 1597, Jehan Lhermite described them thus in his book *Passetemps*: "The first chamber is the waiting room for those who come and go; the second is set aside for ordinary audiences and the third is an excellent drawing room, where His Majesty liked to walk with his children at sunset (...). The fourth is the room where His Majesty normally took his meals (...) and beyond was the door into His Majesty's bedroom."

Marquetry doors, detail.

Zaguán

The first room is the *Pieza de Guardias*, also known as the *Sala de la Silla* (Hall of the Chair), since it is here that the sedan chair is exhibited that Philip II used to make his last journey to San Lorenzo. This interesting piece, designed possibly by Jehan Lhermite himself, consists of a friar's chair the back of which can be lowered by means of a toothed mechanism under the arms. The chair featured awnings that could be lowered to protect the back and the sides.

The *Pieza de Guardias* is a key element within the layout of this part of the building. It has five doors which open into the Queen's Room; the *Piso de Damas;* the Summer Quarters; the King's Room, through the *Patio de Mascarones;* and the Official Rooms.

Outstanding among the decorative elements are the square cloth with the king's arms; the four canvases attributed to Jacopo Bassano, depicting *Noli me Tangere, The Crown of Thorns, Jesus in the House of Martha and Mary* and the *Adoration*

Portrait Hall.

of the Shepherds; and finally the painting attributed to Juan Correa, *The Flagellation of Christ.*

Ambassadors' Room

We continue our itinerary to the Ambassadors' Room, today known as the Hall of Portraits by virtue of the paintings hanging there. Although we have no knowledge of the existence of an iconographical series of portraits in San Lorenzo, we do know that there was one in the Palace of El Pardo, consisting of thirty-seven canvases, most of which were lost in the terrible fire of March 13 1604. The present series is a reconstruction which allows us to see all the monarchs of the House of Austria, beginning with *The Emperor Charles V,* the work of Pantoja de la Cruz and a copy of the original, now lost, by Titian. On either side appear the Emperor's two male offspring, John of Austria, attributed to the same artist, and

Philip II, a masterpiece by Antonio Moro. Next comes the portrait of *Philip III* from the XVII-century Spanish school. Between the windows we encounter *Philip IV as a Child* by Bartolomé González and *Charles II as a Child,* attributed to Juan Carreño de Miranda. The series is completed with portraits of the two wives of Philip IV, *Isabel de Borbón* and *Marian of Austria,* XVIII-century copies on either side of the marquetry door, and *Charles II* next to his mother, *Marian of Austria,* both by Carreño. Above the doors hang *Doña Juana,* Philip II's sister, attributed to Sánchez Coello, and *Philbert of Savoy,* one of Philip II's generals.

The decoration of the room continues with two wooden folding chairs with woven hemp seats. These two pieces were made in China around 1570 (Ming Dynasty) and reached Spain from Manila, where a Spanish trader purchased them as a gift for Philip II. On a simple table from the late XVI century sits the steel drawer in which, according to tradition, the Emperor kept his papers.

The most singular piece in this room is the impressive marquetry door. This work forms part of a set of five doors made in the German city of Augsburg, possibly in the workshop of Bartolomé Weisshaupt, between 1562 and 1568. Tradition has it that they could have been a gift from the Emperor Maximilian II to Philip II who, in 1572, ordered them installed in his quarters in San Lorenzo. The woods used are ash, maple, different coloured walnut, beech and pear. The motifs on the panels are simplified versions of engravings by the Flemish artist Vredeman de Vries.

High Gallery

We now proceed to the High or Main Gallery of the royal quarters, a room in the same style as the *Sala de Batallas.* To its political and recreational use, to which we have already alluded when we spoke of the Hall of Battles, must be added its educational function for, as occurred in the XVI century, above the line of tiles we find, in the words of Father Sigüen-

Galería de Paseo.

Sundial outside the Galería de Paseo.

za, "the descriptions or maps of all the provinces known to us, drawn and graduated by cosmographers and geographers". This collection of maps is the work of Abraham Oertel, known in Spain as Ortelius, who in 1570 published them under the title of *Theatrum orbis terrarum*.

All the paintings are military in theme. On the main wall we find five canvases attributed to Rodrigo de Holanda (Roderick of Holland), with scenes from the Flanders campaign, copies of the frescoes in the *Sala de Batallas*. The remainder of the paintings, with scenes from the same campaign, are from the Flemish school of the early XVII century.

Outstanding among the furniture are the two *bargueños* or Spanish decorated cabinets on legs at both ends of the room, the closed one having been made at the end of the XVI century and the open one early in the XVII.

Encrusted in the floor we contemplate a solar adjuster made by the Hungarian mathematician Juan de Wendlingen in 1755. This instrument was used to set clocks at the correct time.

Finally there are two further marquetry doors, the simplest of the whole set.

Antechamber

Next comes the Antechamber or Dining-Room, a room which was decorated with a multitude of paintings of all sizes, which described the varieties of birds, reptiles and plants found in the Indies, evidence of Philip II's great interest in the natural sciences. Unfortunately none of these have survived, and today the room features a collection of canvases from the Spanish school of the early XVII century describing royal residences and hunting lodges around Madrid. There are views of the palaces of Balsaín, Aranjuez, El Pardo and San Lorenzo, and of Vaciamadrid, Aceca and El Campillo. Next to these is the interesting *Casa de la Nieve* (Snow House), where ice was kept for use in the summer.

Besides these canvases there is a group of engravings by the Flemish artist Pedro Perret on the basis of plans by Juan

155

de Herrera, as is noted in old descriptions of this room. On the floor is a second solar adjuster, also by Wendlingen.

In the antechamber end walls are the two last, and most spectacular, German doors. The one on the gallery side, dated 1567, is considered to be one of the masterpieces of German joinery.

Secretaries' Rooms

Two rooms remain which, though closed to the public, can be contemplated through the doors, and they are known as the *Piezas de los Secretarios* (Secretaries' Rooms), since it is assumed they were used by the king's scribes. These rooms, the floors of which are the oldest in the building (XVII-century), have recently been refurbished and decorated with works from the XVI and XVII centuries.

The smaller of the two is decorated with religious paintings, outstanding among which are *The Annunciation,* from the Flemish school, and *The Rest During the Flight to Egypt,* from the Venetian school, both from the XVI century. On one of the tables is Niccolo dell'Arca's alabaster sculpture of *St. John the Baptist.*

The larger room is decorated with major works of art, outstanding among which are the interesting XVII-century Flemish school *Pelican*; *The Virgin with Child* by Quintin Metsys; *The Money Changer and his Wife* by Marius Reymerswaele; and the portraits, in attitude of prayer, of *Philip IV* and *Marian of Austria,* attributed to Antonio Arias.

On either side of the XVII-century Spanish rug there is an armillary sphere and a lodestone holding a rock of five kilos found near the monastery site.

Finally, mention must be made of the XVII-century Spanish table adorned with marble encrustations representing mythological scenes.

Before entering the King's Chamber we pass through a small room, in the centre of which stands the staircase that forms a pair with the one in the *Pieza de Guardias.* The installation of a long display cabinet on one side of the staircase, designed to ex-

*Philip II's Cuarto Real, general room of the Main Chamber
with the former porcelain exhibition.*

hibit fine earthenware, gives the room the appearance of a passageway. Hanging on its walls are three further views of royal
residences: Monasterio, El Enebral and La Fuenfría. Here we can
also contemplate the interesting pieces of Talavera china made
for the needs of the building's inhabitants. There are inkwells,
vases, plates, cups and salvers, among other objects, which bear
the coat of arms of the prior who commissioned them. The period of the pieces stretches from the XVI to the XVIII centuries.

The Royal Chamber

Having described the official rooms, we now go on to
examine the living quarters, beginning with those of the king.
The Royal Chamber is divided into four rooms: the main
one, the bedroom, the study and the oratory. Their decoration
was originally simple, being limited to religious paintings
and engravings, outstanding among which are those by

Hieronymus van Aeken Bosch (known in Spain as El Bosco), which can now be seen in the Prado Museum. The rooms of Philip II preserve this kind of devotional decoration, contrasting with the simplicity of their walls and white vault and of the plain brick floor.

The main room is presided over by a portrait of *Philip II as an Old Man*, the work of Pantoja's studio, flanked by the busts of his parents (German school, XVI-century). Beneath these paintings there is an ebony altarpiece, in the form of a templet, in the central silver panel of which is a representation of Calvary. The work was designed by Juliano da Porta and made in Rome by Antonio Gentelli Faenza between 1578 and 1585.

Outstanding among the works of art preserved here are the *Landscape with St. Christopher* by Joachim Patinir; the triptych with *Piety* between *St. John the Baptist* and *St. Francis Receiving the Stigmata* by Gerard David; the portable *Christ* sent by Titian to Philip II in 1559 as a gift made by his son Horacio Tiziano (although its great quality makes one suspect it was in fact painted by his father); and *The Virgin with Child Between St. Roque and St. Sebastian*, an original by Benvenuto Garofalo.

Inside the display cabinet in this room we can admire:

First shelf

On the first shelf: Two paintings on agate by Anibal Carracci representing the *Descent from the Cross* and *St. Anthony,* and an anonymous XVI-century bronze bust of Charles I on a marble pedestal.

Second shelf

In the centre of the second shelf, a marble diptych of the "rose" type, so called because the lines dividing the scenes are adorned with these flowers. It is a XVI-century French work and depicts scenes from the life of Jesus Christ. On the left there is a pax tablet in the form of a templet by the silversmith Luis del Castillo from Cuenca. On the right stands a small copper coffer decorated in enamel, made in Limoges during the XII century. It forms part of the series of "St. Thomas Becket" coffers since their fronts show scenes from the martyrdom and burial of the saint.

Third shelf

On the third shelf, starting from the left, is a bone coffer from the late XI century, followed by a German gilt silver amphora from the mid XVI century. The neck is decorated entirely with battle and hunting scenes, while the belly features allegories of taste, touch, war and fidelity. Next comes an image, in coral, of St. Lawrence by Francesco Alferi, showing the saint standing over a fallen king who symbolises heresy. On the base is a fine enamel representation of the fountain of life with two deer drinking from it. On the extreme right we find a gilt bronze aspersorium and aspergillum, from the second half of the XVI century, with the coat of arms of the monastery and the monogram of Philip II.

Fourth and fifth shelves

On the fourth and fifth shelves stands the remainder of the exhibition of the priors' ceramics.

Proceeding into the study, we see "a shelf with books like the ones we have in the cells, of exactly the same quality, and smaller writing desks and chests of drawers", in the words of Father Sigüenza. Decorating the wall facing us is the collection of eleven water-colours attributed to Albrecht Durer and acquired by Philip II.

The most important room, however, and once again quoting the Hieronymite friar, is "the bedroom, the walls of which are covered with small images of saints, so that when the king tossed and turned in bed, (...) wherever he looked he received comfort, seeing himself in such good

View of the Main Altar from the king's bed.

*Clock-oil lamp by Hans de Evalo, made in Madrid in 1583
for Philip II's writing desk.*

company." The decoration of this room remained intact until the Napoleonic invasion, as a result of which all the pieces kept here were dispersed. Part of the collection was retrieved and arranged as we see it today thanks to Carlos Hidalgo, administrator of this Royal Site during the reign of Ferdinand VII. The most interesting object is the bed, which stands in exactly the same spot where at five o'clock on the morning of Saturday, September 13, the king surrendered his soul to God. The XVI-century bed, which stands on a dais of cordovan, is of walnut covered with Flemish tapestries of the same century, the design of which is attributed to Cornelis Floris. It had to be placed so that from it the monarch could see the main altar of the basilica as well as receiving the greatest possible amount of sunlight. The bed in the Royal Bedroom of the Monastery of Yuste also enjoyed this privileged position.

Lastly we come to the oratory, where the king heard mass. This room, between the bedroom and the presbytery, is sumptuously lined in red, white and green marble, and dominated by an altar with a painting of *Christ Bearing the Cross,* an old copy of a work by Titian.

Queen's Chamber

On the opposite side, and following the same layout, is the Royal Chamber used by Prince Philip, the future Philip III, and his sister, the Infanta Isabel Clara Eugenia, hence its present name. The chambers were originally intended for Queen Anne of Austria, Philip II's fourth wife, but her premature death, which occurred in 1580, prevented her from enjoying them.

In the Main Room we contemplate the portraits of *Isabel Clara Eugenia*, attributed to Bartolomé González, and *Catalina Micaela,* by the studio of Sánchez Coello, flanking a portrait of their father, Philip II, by the same studio. Other major works in this room are the XVI-century Italian school panel depicting *The Adoration of the Wise Men, Calvary* by the Flemish painter Frans Vriendt (known as "Floris") and

View of Infanta
Isabel Clara Eugenia's room.

The Triptych of St. Catherine by the circle of the Flem Geerten tot Sint Jans.

In the bedroom there is a simple bed draped with XVI-century Oriental cloths, made possibly in the Philippines. Where the dais formerly was now stands a *realejo* or portable organ of the XVI century with the coat of arms of Philip II on the front. At the far end there is a wax painting of *The Adoration of the Wise Men,* by Brother Eugenio de Torices, and to our left, on a table, a *Descent* in ivory, a Flemish work from the second half of the XVI century.

Patio *of Masks*

During our initerary through the different rooms of the palace we have seen an inner patio known as the *Patio de los Mascarones* (Patio of Masks) This singular courtyard was

"Adoration of the Wise Men", by Torices.

Patio *of Masks*

designed by Juan Bautista de Toledo with three arched cloister galleries on columns on the first floor; the fourth of these galleries has been altered, and now has blind arches on pilasters. The centres of the arches have niches containing two fountains, and the water emerges from spouts in the form of masks. The patio follows the traditional style, with balconies on the second floor and windows on the third.

The Painting Museum

The Painting Museum corresponds to the rooms situated below the Royal Quarters, whose original purpose was to provide the monarchs with a second set of living quarters for the summer months. Their numerous offspring, however, meant that this Royal Site was always rather small, making it difficult to accommodate them on the first floor and lofts. As a result, these rooms were soon occupied by by the Infantes and people of confidence who accompanied them.

The rooms are arranged in exactly the same way as on the first floor and, after they had been restored, it was decided to use them as a painting museum.

Our itinerary begins at the two rooms situated in the gallery of the Royal Patio, which were also restored on the occasion of the IV Centenary of the building, which formed part of the series of reception rooms.

The Antechamber of Honour

The visit to the museums of San Lorenzo begins with one of the foremost pieces of late XVI[!]-century Spanish statuary, namely *St. Michael Defeating the Devil* by Luisa Roldán, known as "La Roldana". This sculpture was ordered by Charles II in 1692, and the polychrome is the work of Tomás de los Arcos, the artist's brother-in-law. On the strength of this work, Luisa Roldán was appointed chamber sculptress.

The decoration of this room is completed with two tapestries, the first of which, *The Tribulations of Life on Earth,* is no. 3 in series no. 36 of the National Heritage tapestry collection titled *The Temptations of St. Anthony.* The subject is inspired in Bosch's *The Hay Cart* which, as we have seen, is also in this monastery.

On the opposite wall hangs tapestry no. 1 in series no. 1 of the National Heritage collection, titled *The Triumphs of the Mother of God* or, alternatively, *Golden Tapestries.* The title of this particular work is *God Sends the Angel Gabriel to the Virgin Mary;* at the top we see the Holy Trinity as three crowned kings, between Mercy and Justice, who send Gabriel with his message to Mary, seen at the bottom, reading and surrounded by figures. The composition is completed with scenes from the Old Testament which prefigure this mystery of salvation.

The Chamber of Honour

This room is presided over by the magnificent *Martyrdom of St. Mauricius and the Theban Legion* by Domenicos Theotocopoulos, otherwise known as El Greco. Mauricius, an officer in the Roman army, was executed on September 22 285 for disobeying Emperor Maximian's orders to attack the Gauls, who had recently been converted to Christianity. In the foreground we see the saint accompanied by Exuperius and Candidus at the moment when, faithful to their own religious beliefs, they refuse the invitation on the part of the imperial emissary to worship the Roman gods. At the top there is an opening in the background which depicts the Glory of Heaven, with angels bearing the palms and crowns of the martyrs. The work is completed in the middle distance, where we see the execution of the soldiers who formed the Theban legion.

In this room hang the remainder of the pieces forming the *Golden Tapestries* series, a collection purchased by Queen Juana on August 10 1502 from the Flemish weaver Pierre van Aelst. It is believed that the cartoons were by Quintin Metsys.

The following tapestry depicts *The Annunciation*. In the centre appear Jesus Christ and Mary, whom the angel approaches in order to give her his message, surrounded by feminine figures representing the Virtues. The composition is completed with scenes from the Old Testament.

The third tapestry depicts *The Birth of Christ,* together with the *Adoration of the Wise Men* and *Jesus among the Doctors.* At the top appear scenes from the Old Testament.

The series is completed with *The Coronation of the Virgin* by the Holy Trinity, surrounded by the Virtues. Next to the scenes from the Old Testament are two representing the *Coro-*

nation of a Young Girl and *Delivery of a Portrait to a Lady*, which might allude to the coronation of Doña Juana as Queen of Castile and to the introduction to her fiancé, King Philip.

The Summer Palace

Hall No. I: Italian Painting

In this first hall, directly below the Chambers of the Infanta Isabel Clara Eugenia, there is a collection of Italian works from the XVI and XVII centuries, outstanding among which are those from the Venetian school:

St. Margaret, attributed to Titian, depicts the saint at the moment when she miraculously emerges from the belly of the dragon that had devoured her.

Virgin of Sorrows, copy of a work by Titian. This painting is on slate, which confers upon it its peculiar texture.

The Eternal Father and the Holy Ghost by Paolo Veronese, one of this painter's masterpieces preserved in San Lorenzo. It presides over the cell of Father Sigüenza.

The Descent from the Cross, attributed to Carletto Veronese. With a number of variations, it follows the patterns established by his father, Paolo Veronese.

The Descent from the Cross, a larger copy of the previous work by Carletto Veronese.

The Adoration of the Wise Men, attributed to Carletto Veronese although, by virtue of the great quality of certain parts of the work, it could be an original by his father.

The Adoration of the Wise Men, attributed to Carletto Veronese. This canvas is a smaller replica of an original by this master, recently attributed to his palette.

The Conversion of Magdalene, attributed to Domenico Tintoretto. The saint, stripped of all her wealth, kneels in an imploring attitude.

Ecce Homo, a somewhat later version of a subject created by Titian.

The Archangel St. Michael, attributed to Luca Cambiaso.
The Virgin of Sorrows, a copy by Massimo Stanzione.
Mary Magdalene at Prayer by Lucas Jordán.

Hall No. II: Flemish Painting

The second hall is given over to Flemish painting from the XVI and XVII centuries.

The Seven Liberal Arts, attributed to Martin de Vos. As in the Library, each Art is accompanied by its respective symbols.

The Judgment of Solomon, a work dated 1562 and which might be an early work by either Joachim Beuckelaer or Pieter Aerstsen.

The Supper at Emaus, a high-quality copy of the original by Rubens, formerly property of the monastery and at present exhibited in the Prado Museum.

The Immaculate Conception, a late copy of an original by Rubens which, like the previous work, was once the property of the monastery and is now in the Prado.

The Virgin Mary with the Child, an excellent copy of a canvas by Anton van Dyck.

The Holy Family, copy of another work by van Dyck by the XIX- century Spanish school.

Piety by the Flemish school.

The Martyrdom of St. Justine by Lucas Jordán in imitation of the style of Veronese. It is therefore the only non-Flemish work in the hall.

Hall No. III: Michel Coxcie

This hall is devoted entirely to the work of the Flemish painter Michel Coxcie, known among his contemporaries by the nickname of the "Flemish Raphael". Coxcie was court painter to the Emperor Charles V, for whom he produced religious paintings, portraits, cartoons for tapestries and designs for stained-glass windows. Philip II held him in high esteem, commissioning him to produce a great number of works for San Lorenzo.

The Immaculate Conception, an interesting version of this Marian theme. The special form of the panel is due to the fact that it is the only altarpiece lacking in the basilica.

The Martyrdom of St. Philip, an impressive triptych, in the central panel of which the saint appears at the moment of his martyrdom.

David and Goliath. This panel depicts the moment when the triumphant David is about to cut off the head of the Philistine giant.

The Genealogy of Jesus Christ. In the centre of the composition appears the Virgin Mary with the Child Jesus surrounded by relatives. This iconography is typical of the Flemish world.

Christ Bearing the Cross. This is almost certainly the painting that, under the title of *The Street of Bitterness,* Charles V took with him to his retreat in the Monastery of Yuste.

The Last Supper, a work attributed to this master.

The Annunciation and *The Birth of Jesus,* by a Flemish school very close to Coxcie. These two works are considered to be two of the panels of a triptych which has since been lost. The central panel would have been *The Adoration of the Wise Men.*

Hall No. IV: Masterpieces

The Promenade Gallery of the Summer Palace was decorated with Luca Cambiasso's six large canvases representing *The Battle of Lepanto.* These works are now exhibited in the gallery of the Palace Patio.

Calvary. A masterpiece of XV-century Flemish painting, commissioned from Roger van der Weyden for the Carthusian monastery of Scheut. The panel representing Christ on the Cross, between the Virgin Mary and St. John, might have been purchased personally by Philip II during his journey through the Netherlands in 1555.

The Descent from the Cross, a copy by Michel Coxcie of the original by Roger van der Weyden, now in the Prado Museum.

The Annunciation by Paolo Veronese and *The Adoration of the Shepherds* by Jacopo Tintoretto. These two canvases were commissioned by Philip II for the main altar of the basilica, which explains their large, elongated size. Although the works were to the king's liking, however, they did not satisfy his iconographical demands, and for this reason were never hung in the church.

The pictorial decoration was entrusted to Federico Zúccaro, who produced the whole set of works. Unfortunately, the arrogance of his character prevented his work from being appreciated as it deserved, a fact illustrated by the cases of his *The Adoration of the Shepherds* and *The Adoration of the Wise Men,* canvases replaced on the altarpiece by others on the same theme by Tibaldi.

The foremost Spanish painter to work in San Lorenzo was Juan Fernández Navarrete, known as "El Mudo" (the Mute). As well as the set of paintings he produced for the lesser altars in the basilica, outstanding among his works is this collection of six canvases, destined mostly to adorn the main high cloister: *The Birth of Our Lord and the Adoration of the Shepherds, The Holy Family, The Flagellation of Christ, The Beheading of St. James, The Burial of St. Lawrence* and *St. Jerome Doing Penance.*

The Vocation of St. Andrew and St. Peter is described by Father Sigüenza as a "brave" work, by virtue of the "beautiful and ordered treatment of the composition".

The Baptism of Christ and *St. Jerome Doing Penance,* by Jacopo Palma "Il Giovane", were acquired by Philip II in order to decorate the chapter rooms.

The last work in this hall is *Christ Bearing the Cross* by Giovan Francesco Guercino.

Hall No. V: Spanish Painting

This hall is given over to XVII-century Spanish painting. We begin with *The Annunciation* by Bartolomé Carducho, a *madrileño* even though he was born in Florence, and continue with *The Immaculate Conception*, produced in the studio of Francisco Pacheco.

The artist best represented here is José de Ribera, by whom we can contemplate portraits of the philosopher *Crisipus* and the author of fables *Aesop*, as well as religious compositions such as *St. Jerome Doing Penance* and *The Child Jesus Appears to St. Anthony of Padua*.

From the Madrid school we can admire *The Annunciation* by Francisco Rizzi, *The Birth of the Virgin* by Jusepe Leonardo and *St. Bárbara*, the work of an anonymous painter.

The work of Francisco Zurbarán is represented by *The Presentation of the Virgin in the Temple*, from the Convent of the Calced Trinity of Seville; we finish with *David Triumphant* by José Montiel, a Spanish master still relatively unknown, and the anonymous *San Pedro de Alcántara*.

Hall No. VI: Spanish and Italian Painting. XVI and XVII Centuries

Our itinerary through this hall begins with the Spanish copy of Daniele de Volterra's *The Assumption of the Virgin*. *The Tears of St. Peter* and *St. Peter in Attitude of Prayer* are clear examples of the force of the models created by José de Ribera, widely copied by his studio.

By Alonso Cano we have two versions of *The Virgin and Child*, and next come further examples of the work of the Madrid school: *St. Philip*, attributed to Sebastián de Herrera Barnuevo, who besides being court painter was also the curator of San Lorenzo; *St. Jerome Whipped by the Angels* and *Mary Magdalene, Penitent* by Diego Polo; and finally *St. Jerome in Attitude of Prayer* by Matías Torres.

The Italian school is represented by an anonymous XVI-century *Descent from the Cross* and the copy of *St. Peter*, the original of which is by Giovan Francesco Guercino. Predominant here is the work of Lucas Jordán, with *Jesus of Nazareth* a processional stage from Ocaña (Toledo), *The Birth of Christ*,

Noli me Tangere, The Doubts of St. Thomas and *St. Jerome in Attitude of Prayer*.

Hall No. VII: Spanish, Italian and Flemish Painting

The first work we encounter is the portrait of *Queen Marian of Austria*, Philip II's second wife, attributed to the studio of Claudio Coello.

The Italian school is represented by portraits of *St. Augustin* and *St. Monica;* the interesting portrait of *Pope Innocent X and a Prelate*, painted in 1654 by Pietro Martire Neri; *Jacob's Journey* by Andrea de Lione; a portrait of *Charles II* attributed to Lucas Jordán; and *Allegory of Life* and *Allegory of Death,* anonymous works from the late XVI century.

We conclude our visit with *Game of Angels and Animals,* a canvas that imitates XVII-century Flemish models.

Hall No. VIII: Flowers and Still Lifes

In this hall we find interesting examples of this genre of painting from the XVII to the XIX centuries. Representing the Spanish school are two still lifes signed by Juan van der Homen y León, an early XVII-century Madrid artist, which depict small birds pecking at fruit. From the XVIII century are four canvases of fruit and kitchen utensils on a table, signed by Luis Meléndez, another Madrid artist who shone in this genre. From the end of this century are the two flower vases attributed to the Valencian Benito Espinés and the two canvases of dead fowl probably by López Enguidanos, who also hailed from Valencia. Sánchez Ramos' still life of two dead fowl dates from 1856.

The Italian school is represented here by *Dead Partridges,* the work of Mariano Neri, a Neapolitan painter who settled in Madrid in 1759, while from the Flemish school there are two flower vases by Daniel Seghers, a still life of the hunt by Peter Boel and a kitchen still life by Jaris van Son.

Hall No. IX: Italian Painting from the XVI, XVII and XVIII Centuries

The last hall in the Painting Museum is given over to the Italian school. The first work is on copper and was found on the roof of the Prior's Tower when the monastery roofs were replaced. It represents *The Virgin Mary and the Child with St. John* and is attributed to Romanelli. The next work is Giovan Francesco Guercino's *Lot Inebriated by his Daughters*, an excellent canvas which Cardinal Ludovisi made as a gift to Philip IV. These are followed by Daniele Crespi's *St. Peter Contemplating Jesus Christ*, a copy of Giovanni Battista Salvi Sassoferrato's *The Virgin*, made by his son, and *St. John as a Child* and *St. Christopher*, both anonymous works.

From the Neapolitan school we have Artemisia Gentileschi's *The Virgin of the Rosary*, acquired by Queen Elisabeth Farnese; *The Adoration of the Wise Men* by Pietro Novelli; *The Sacrifice of Noah* from the XVII-century Neapolitan school; and a copy of *The Adoration of the Wise Men* by Lucas Jordán.

The Museum of Architecture

The Museum of Architecture was created in 1963 as part of the exhibition held to commemorate the IV Centenary of the placing of the first stone on the vault floor of the palace. The museum has now reopened its doors with a new layout of exhibits, to which have been added some of the elements from the exhibition that the Ministry of Public Works organised in 1986 to commemorate the placing of the last stone of the monastery.

The exhibition currently consists of two areas:

- The first, divided into eight halls, where the conception and creation of the monastery is explained, and

Architecture Museum:
Machinery Gallery.

- the second, divided into five halls, where a selection of the materials, tools and machinery used for its construction is displayed.

Hall No. I: The Precedents to and Origin of the "Idea"

In this hall a wide selection of plans of Spanish religious foundations is on display. We begin with those that combine religious and funerary functions, such as the Church of Isidoro in León, the pantheon of the monarchs of León, and the Monastery of Poblet, the pantheon of the Aragonese sovereigns. Next come the plans for hospital buildings (those of Granada and of Santa Cruz in Toledo), whose layout in the form of a cross might have influenced the conception of San Lorenzo. Other buildings represented here are the Alcázar and the Martos Prison, both in Toledo. Together with these exhibits is a a facsimile copy of the first Spanish edition of Serlio's architectural work, dedicated to Philip II when he was still Prince of Asturias.

After passing the maquette of the monastery, by León Gil de Palacios, we come to the next hall.

Hall No. II: Juan Bautista de Toledo: the "Universal Plan"

The different plans, models and maquettes displayed here show the initial projects which Toledo presented to Philip II. Together with these drawings, we see the ground plans of two Hieronymite monasteries: Guadalupe (Cáceres) and El Parral (Segovia). The exhibits are completed with two topographical surveys of the site chosen for the construction of the monastery.

On one of the walls we contemplate the 1963 fresco by Vaquero Turcios which depicts Philip II holding a rose, the symbol of architecture, with Herrera, Villacastín, Trezzo and Arias Montano.

Hall No. III: Juan de Herrera: The Realisation of the Project

After Toledo's death in 1567, Juan de Herrera took charge of the work until it was finished, and the sight of the completed building was recorded for posterity by the Flemish engraver Pedro Perret. In the centre of the hall stands the large maquette which shows the state of the building according to Hatfield's drawing, a copy of which can be seen in hall no. XI of this museum.

Hall No. IV: The Development of the Project: the Plans in the Palace Library

This hall exhibits the plans for the construction of San Lorenzo contained in the palace library. In the centre are the original remains of the roofing of the *Torre de las Damas*.

Hall No. V: El Escorial and Spanish Architecture of the XVI and XVII Centuries

Having examined the collection of plans, the visitor is able to contemplate the work done on the monastery during the XVII century: the Royal Pantheon and the Altar of the Sacred Form. In the centre the maquettes are exhibited of the staircase and the capitals.

Hall No. VI: El Escorial and XVIII-Century Spanish Architectural Culture

With the arrival of Charles III, the Royal Site of San Lorenzo was founded and the monastery was integrated into the urban complex whose layout was designed by Juan de Villanueva. This new image was recorded in prints by López Enguidanos, on the basis of drawings by Gómez de Navia, and by Asselinau, from paintings by Brambilla. Exhibited in the hall are the original remains of the Monument to Holy Week, built by Juan de Herrera, and a maquette of the same monument made in the workshops of the P.N. (???)

Gallery of tools and machinery

This gallery is divided into five areas where it is possible to contemplate a large exhibition of the tools, materials, crafts and machinery used both in the construction and the maintenance of the building.

Hall No. VII

We begin with the tools, among which are *espadones de cantero*, special trowels used to spread the mortar between ashlars; *batidoras* or beaters for preparing the lime; *llagueros* for cleaning the joins; *paletas* or trowels for spreading the lime; *sierras* or saws for cutting wood; *cazos*, special cauldrons for melting metal; *punteros* or pointed chisels for working stone; *brocas* or drill bits for probing the ground; *escantillones* to draw the lines and fix the dimensions of the ashlars; the utensils for a lime kiln: *horquillas* (forks), *picos* (picks), *pinchos* (pointed instruments) and *rastrillos* (rakes); *agujas*, needles for alignments; and *pisones* for setting stones in position.

Hall No. VIII

We now continue with materials, namely granite from the mountains of Madrid and Avila, bricks for construction and decoration, tiles for socles, skirtings and rooms, and slate for the roofing.

Hall No. IX

This hall is devoted to carpentry, which in San Lorenzo reached such heights of perfection that it could be considered cabinetmaking. Especially outstanding here are the model for the spire for the Torre de las Damas, made using the original woods, and the paneled window-shutters.

Hall No. X

Other crafts are represented in this exhibition, among them locksmithing, lead roofing, stained-glass window making and silversmithing.

Hall No. XI

In this, the last of the halls, we find a reproduction of the foundation stone, the original of which is beneath the prior's chair in the refectory; a reproduction of the drawing attributed to Fabrizio Castello, showing a view of the monastery during its construction. The original is the property of Lord Salisbury and is kept in Hatfield, London. Together with these two works there is a mock-up of the *pluma* (feather), the crane designed by Herrera to lift the ashlars.

The Palace of the Bourbons

As was to be expected, a building so significant for the Habsburg dynasty could hardly be to the liking of the new Bourbon sovereigns, recognised as the Spanish monarchs after the Peace of Utrecht, signed in 1713, which put an end (except in Catalonia) to the War of Succession. Indeed, it was not until the reign of Charles III, which began in 1759, that San Lorenzo became frequented once again by the Court. Although the first Bourbon monarch, Philip IV,

Salón Pompeyano. Detail.

was much enamoured of this residence, he did nothing to enhance its distinction, since during his reign artistic attention was focused on the construction of the *Palacio Nuevo* in Madrid and the Palace of San Ildefonso in the province of Segovia.

With the ascent to the throne of Charles III, formerly ruler of the Kingdom of Naples, the situation of the building changed radically after the establishment of the system of *Jornadas Reales* (king's stays in royal residences). The monarch's life was organised around five palaces, in each of which he lived for some months of the year, and one of these was San Lorenzo. Until 1764, when the *Palacio Nuevo* was inaugurated, the king's official residence was the Palace of El Buen Retiro, where he spent Christmas. After Epiphany he moved to the Royal Site of El Pardo, during Holy Week he stayed in Madrid and then went to Aranjuez until the beginning of the hot season, when the royal family moved to San Ildefonso, the only Bourbon foundation.

At the beginning of September, the Court was transferred to San Lorenzo, where it would stay until mid November, finally returning once again to the capital to celebrate Christmas.

Charles III marked this rigid, monotonous way of life, causing the creation of floating populations which, with the passing of time, became permanent settlements. Thus, on May 3 1767 the Royal Order was signed that lifted Philip II's ban on building around the monastery and the Royal Site of San Lorenzo was created, the document making it perfectly clear that the buildings constructed could be occupied only when the Court was in residence; the rest of the year they had to remain vacant.

However, it was during the reign of his successor, Charles IV, that the architectural work was carried out that would radically alter the structure of the monastery, in order to repair the damage caused to the royal chambers by a fire which occurred in 1786. The mission was entrusted to the royal architect, Juan de Villanueva, who concentrated his efforts on:

- Substituting the heavy vaults of the first floor for much lighter arches of brick laid on the flat;

- Modifying the openings on the northern façade, in order to facilitate direct access for carriages to the *Patio de Coches* (Coach Patio), and finally

- Constructing a new main staircase.

The part of the monastery we know today as the Palace of the Bourbons corresponds to the Royal Quarters used by Charles IV and María Luisa de Parma.

The main staircase

Our itinerary begins at the staircase built by Juan de Villanueva, which was required to lead from the ground to the first floors. Due to the considerable height between, the flight had to make two about-turns, with a wide landing between, so that climbing it would be as easy as possible. Its decoration today consists basically of paintings. On the landing we have the portraits of Charles IV and his wife, María Luisa de Parma, a replica by Goya's studio. On the first floor we contemplate the interesting canvas attributed to Felipe de Silva, which depicts Philip V accompanied by Faith killing a dragon that tramples overturned goblets, scattered wafers, crucifixes and missals. Opposite is his first wife, María Luisa Gabriel and the Prince of Asturias, the future Luis I. In the background we see the Monastery of San Lorenzo and the Virgin of Patronage, between St. Jerome and St. Lawrence. The painting is an allegory of the first Bourbon king putting sin to death.

The remainder of the works are landscapes, except for the fourth one, by Francisco Sasso, depicting *St. James Serving Soup to the Destitute*.

Our itinerary begins in three small rooms in which Char-

Hunting Scene with the Monarchs of Naples,
bisque from Capodimonte.

les IV had his studio. Their present-day decoration has nothing to do with the original one of the XVIII century.

Hall No. I

This hall is decorated with an interesting selection of landscapes, most of which belonged to the *Casita del Príncipe* (Prince's little house). Outstanding among them are the *View of Venice* from the XVII-century Italian school and *A Fortress Besieged* by Spolverini.

Hall No. II

This hall is presided over by an impressive bisque porcelain piece made in Capodimonte (Naples) in 1781 and depic-

Chinero: view of the sideboard.

ting Ferdinand IV and María Carolina in a hunting scene. Above there are a further two portraits of the same monarchs, also in porcelain. The remainder of the hall is decorated with feminine portraits, the work of Rosalba Carriera except for the one of Henrietta of England, now attributed to Jean Nocret.

Hall No. III

The third of these rooms is decorated with XVIII- century Spanish painting, outstanding among which is Mariano Salvador Maella's *St. Paschal.*

After crossing the passageway that separates the rooms looking outwards from those looking onto the patio, we reach a large hall, known today as the *Chinero* (china cabinet), which in the XVIII century formed part of the royal work-

shops. Its name alludes to the interesting china cabinet in which a set of crockery from the porcelain collection of the National Heritage is displayed. This particular service was made in 1905 in Copeland (England) and came to Spain as part of the trousseau of Queen Victoria Eugenia de Battemberg, when she married Alphonso XIII in 1906. Each element is of white porcelain decorated with peacocks in different colours and with cobalt blue trimming. On the walls of this room hang Lucas Jordán's canvases representing *Apollo and Marsias* and *Athenea and Arachne;* a work by Giovanni Lanfranco, *The Triumph of a Roman Emperor;* and a copy by Francisco de los Santos of Raphael's *Battle of the Milvius Bridge.*

Pieza de Trucos

Our itinerary through the official halls begins in a large room, today the Gala Dining Room and formerly the *Pieza de Trucos,* since it was here that the royal family gathered to play trucks, the antecedent to the modern game of billiards. The wall decoration is the same throughout the whole set of rooms: framed tapestries.

The tapestry is one of the most important decorative elements used by European courts during the XVIII century. Following this trend, the House of Bourbon established their own factory, founded by Philip V who, in 1720, summoned Jacobo van der Goten to set it in motion. The *Real Fábrica de Tapices de Santa Bárbara* began to function the folowing year, its main client being the Royal House. The technique of tapestry manufacture demands the presence of painters who design the cartoons or models on the basis of which the weavers work. At first the cartoonists restricted themselves to copying the works of great masters, until Antonio Rafael Mengs, Charles III's court painter, decided to foster *costumbrista* painting, that is, painting that depicts everyday life and prevalent customs, creating cartoons showing the festivals and types of XVIII-

Dining-Room Antechamber.

century Madrid and producing original works to serve as models.

The ceilings of these rooms are the work of Vicente Gómez and his studio, and constitute the earliest examples of neoclassical decoration promoted by Charles III in San Lorenzo, by request of the Prince of Asturias, since work began in 1772. The elements employed were essentially small canopies, renaissance in outline, together with Pompeian and Roman motifs.

Presiding over the main wall of the first room are three tapestries representing *The Ball on the Banks of the Manzanares,* based on a cartoon by Goya, *The Ball near the Bridge over the Manzanares Canal* and *The Paseo de las Delicias,* by the Bayeu brothers. Above one of the doors there are also *The Engagement* by Goya, *Afternoon Tea in the Country* by the Bayeus and *The Fox Hunt* by Antonio del Castillo.

Antechamber

We now proceed to the Antechamber or *Aparador,* a small waiting room with tapestries based on the works of David Teniers and Philips Wouwerman, Flemish artists from the XVII century.

Ambassadors' Ante-Room

In the next hall, called the Ambassadors' Ante-Room, we can admire the best selection of tapestries based on models by Goya. First of all we have *The Paseo de Andalucía,* also known as *Lady and Muffled Figures, The Kite, The Card Players* and, above the door, *Boys Gathering Fruit,* all produced between 1776 and 1778. Between 1779 and 1780 Goya designed *The Crockery Seller* and *The Washerwomen,* and in 1792 *The Small Giants, Boys Climbing a Tree,* and *The Seesaw,* each one above a door. The tapestry collection contained in this room is completed by the Bayeu brothers' *El Paseo de las Delicias.*

Ambassadors' Ante-Room.

Ambassadors' Room

At the northern end we come finally to the Ambassadors' Room or *Salón de Corte*, a large hall decorated with tapestries based on cartoons by the Bayeu brothers, depicting popular scenes such as *The Muleteer and the Gardener*, *The Game of Bowls*, *"Majos" Playing Cards* and the famous *Pedro Rico the Sausage Maker*. Next to these drapes we have others reflecting the world of childhood: *Children Playing at Bullfighters*, *Children's Kitchen* (also called *Christmas Night*) and *The Little Girl with a Pushcart*. The ceiling is in imitation panelwork, in the central section of which appear angels showing the coat of arms of Charles III.

The King's Quarters

At the southern end we come across the first two rooms of the King's Quarters: the Antechamber with its small Oratory, and the king's former office, known today as the Second Salon of Telemachus. The walls of these two rooms are covered with some of the tapestries that form the series *The Adventures of Young Telemachus, Son of Ulysses*, inspired by the book by François Salignac de la Mothe Fénelon, tutor to the Duke of Burgundy, the granson of Louis XIV. In these tapestries, woven in Brussels in 1729 by Daniel and Urban Leynier on the basis of cartoons by an unknown painter, we follow some of the adventures of this youth from Ancient Greece as he goes in search of his father. In the XVII century Telemachus was taken as the pedagogical and political model for the education of illustrious princes, since he symbolises man's aspiration to know, think and give opinions according to the dictates of reason.

Outstanding in the Antechamber is the drape, on both sides of the mantelpiece, depicting the encounter between Telemachus and his tutor, Nestor, and the nymph Calypso, which was added to the series by special request of the king. The tapestry was produced in Madrid between 1751 and

Second Room of Telemachus.

1753, based on a cartoon by Miguel Angel Houasse, Philip V's court painter. Presiding over the altar is Lucas Jordán's *The Holy Family*, together with a XVII-century Spanish ivory crucifix.

Another tapestry from the same series hangs in the old office and represents Neptune, together with the nymph Calypso, calming the storm which is about to sink the ship in which Telemachus is sailing. The scene is taken from chapter five of the book of Telemachus.

Princess' Quarters

Proceeding to the Princess' Quarters, we begin at the Entrance Room, decorated with tapestries cynegetic in theme. Outstanding among these are the drapes based on drawings by the Bayeu brothers, depicting *The Boar Hunt* and *The Deer Hunt*, together with the one based on a cartoon by Ginés Andrés de Aguirre, inspired in the work of Wouwerman, representing *Departure for the Hunt*. An elegant crystal lamp from La Granja hangs from the ceiling.

Wet Nurses' Room

The next room also belongs to the Princess' Quarters, and was formerly known as the Wet Nurses' Room; today it is known as the *Salón Pompeyano* by virtue of the tapestries it contains, the cartoons for which are attributed to José del Castillo. The motifs represented are medallions in imitation blue marble with feminine figures in white, beneath elegant canopies and accompanied by a great number of decorative elements that constitute a wide repertoire of Pompeian motifs.

Queen's Quarters

Finally we arrive at the Queen's Quarters, beginning our visit in the entrance vestibule to the *Sala de Corte*. Hanging in

Salón Pompeyano.

this room are tapestries by Goya, such as *The Brawl in the New Tavern*, *The "Novillada"* (fight with young bulls) and above the doors *Boys Blowing Up Bladders* and *The Shepherd Boy*; and by the Bayeu brothers, such as *The Tied Bull*, also known as *The Bull Festival in Carabanchel*, and *Departure for the Deer Hunt*; finally there is Castillo's *The Gardens of El Retiro from the Bronze Horse Enclosure*.

Usher's Room

Next comes the Usher's Room, for the queen's servant who controlled the comings and goings to and from her chambers. The room is hung with tapestries cynegetic in theme, among which are two by Goya, *The Fisherman* and *Hunter Loading his Shotgun*, and one by Aguirre, representing *Departure for the Hunt with Falcons*.

Antechamber

The last of the queens chambers included in this visit to the palace is the Antechamber. This room, decorated with tapestries inspired by the work of Teniers, communicates directly with the *Sala de Batallas*. Note the fine tapestry over the door, *Hounds on the Leash*, based on a cartoon by Goya.

Eastern façade

Our description now continues with the rooms along the eastern façade which overlook the gardens, although they are not included in this itinerary through the palace. The Queen's Quarters are completed with the *Sala de Corte*, today known as the Music Room by virtue of the musical instruments it contains, the first of which is a harp manufactured by Holtzaman in Paris during the first third of the XIX

Pieza de Paso, with Goya's "The Brawl in the New Tavera".

century. The second is an English piano, from the same period, built by Thomas Tomkinson. Outstanding among the tapestries are *The Quail Hunt* and *The Game of Pelota,* based on cartoons by Goya, and Castillo's *Promenade beside the Lake in El Retiro.*

Next to this room is the queen's oratory, presided over by a painting depicting *The Virgin Mary and the Child between a Saint and an Angel,* a copy of the original by the Florentine painter Andrea del Sarto.

We now proceed to the former boudoir, which is now a private dining room, decorated with a second, inverted version of Goya's *The Game of Pelota* and *The Alcalá Gate and Cibeles Fountain* by Ginés Andrés de Aguirre. The ceiling can be considered one of Vicente Gómez's masterpieces.

The Royal Chambers finish with the Queen's Bedroom, with another original ceiling by Gómez. Outstanding among the tapestries exhibited here is the one over the door, *Children with a Mastiff,* based on a cartoon by Goya, and *"Valencianos" Making a Paella* by the Bayeu brothers.

The Princess' Quarters now continue with the Recreation Room, containing the Boudoir, with two large tapestries featuring popular scenes based on cartoons by Castillo *(Beggars Pleading for Alms)* and Antonio Barbaza *(The Pilgrimage).*

We proceed to the bedroom, decorated with tapestries such as *The Gate of San Vicente* and a new version of *The Alcalá Gate and Cibeles Fountain,* based on cartoons by Aguirre.

Finally we must mention the rooms forming the King's Quarters: the Oval Room, with Pompeian theme tapestries by Castillo, and the Dressing Room, today known as the Gothic Salon, with three tapestries by Goya -*The Boar Hunt, Spring,* and, over the door, *The Lady and the Soldier*- and one by Castillo, *The Return from the Hunt.* Another interesting feature of this room is the furniture, made in pear wood and inspired in Gothic forms.

We terminate our description by mentioning the famous set of rooms called the Rooms of Fine Wood -office, private room, ante-oratory and oratory- located between the eastern and northern façades beneath the *Torre de las Damas.* They were

begun during the reign of Charles IV, around 1794, and, after a series of interruptions, completed by Angel Maeso in 1831. The name alludes to the fact that they are entirely of fine woods -flooring, friezes, windows, shutters, doors and mouldings-, constituting one of the finest contributions to this art from XVIII-century Spain.

The first room to be finished was the oratory, for which hurunday, jará, palosanto, lapancho, lignum vitae, cedar, ebony, terebinth and other woods were used. The composition, which follows French models, features a marquetry socle above which are placed vertical panels, with silk decoration by Camille Pernon from Lyon, notable among which are the doors, windows, mirror and prie-dieu, covered with marquetry. The floor decoration is similar, with a central rosette formed from Greek palms and acanthus leaves. The ceiling was decorated by Vicente Gómez and constitutes an allegory of Faith surrounded by the figures of Charity, Fortitude, Hope and Wisdom. Notable here also is the furniture, above all the console and the prie-dieu by virtue of their bronze lamps, the work of Domingo Urquiza.

Following in descending order of importance are the office, the ante-oratory and the private room which, although built during the reign of Ferdinand VII, present the same unity of style as the oratory, since they were designed before the French invasion. The office follows the same concept of vertical bands on a marquetry socle adorned with landscapes on copper by Bartolomé Moltavo. The silks are bordered by a rich border of plant motifs, probably by Pernon. The ceiling, again the work of Vicente Gómez, features a circular composition on the basis of medallions with figures against blue and red backgrounds, surrounding ovals with cherubim heads. The most spectacular work, however, is the work desk which, following French models, can be closed without the need to put away the documents on top. The design is attributed to Juan de Villanueva.

With these rooms we conclude our visit to the Palace of the Bourbons.

Rooms of Fine Wood: Oratory.

Office of Fine Woods.

*Detail of the wall decoration with
the Montalvo coppers.*

Smaller College Patio.

7.- COLLEGE AND SEMINARY

Following the same layout of the monastery, at the northern end of the building we come across the area used as
the college and seminary, today referred to as the *Colegio de
Alfonso XII*. In the original design, by Juan Bautista de Toldeo,
this area was destined for the palace services, but when the
decision was made to include these activities in the life of San
Lorenzo, the layout had to be modified, although the symmetrical structure was respected. Next to the kitchens, refectory,
toilets, bedrooms and skylight, Juan de Herrera had to arran-
ge the classrooms and a wide inner room of passage which
the students used on rainy days or when the weather was
cold.

*View of the back of the Monastery
from the Gardens*

8.- GARDENS

T he Monastery of San Lorenzo is bordered by gardens to the south and east. Visits are today restricted to the one called the *Jardín de los Frailes* (Friars' Garden), which runs along the southern façade, from which one of the finest views from the building can be enjoyed. Following on from this are the *Jardines Privados* (Private Gardens) on the eastern side, divided into compartments by granite walls crowned with herreriana balls.

Philip II was a nature enthusiast; it is therefore hardly surprising that he should have included it so prominently in the plans for the building. On the one hand, we have the garden, or humanised and ordered vision of nature whose purpose is to provide visual pleasure; on the other, the vegetable garden and the *bosquecillo* (small wood), destined for productivity. The two areas are linked by six stairways dividing into two at the top.

The great variety of flowers endowed this part of the building with "great joyfulness", and its beauty and multitude of colours was compared to the rugs brought back from Turkey or Damascus. According to Juan Alonso de Almela, the court physician, up to sixty-eight different varieties of flowers were planted, of all colours and perfumes, most of them with medicinal properties, which gave this plantation the category of *re-jardín*. Together with this great collection, a genuine botanical garden, over four-hundred plant species were sent from the New World by the doctor and naturalist Francisco Hernando, with which Brother Juan de San Jerónimo composed a collection of pictures to decorate the Antechamber or king's dining-room.

The Gallery of Convalescents

Included from the very beginning in the monastery project were plans for another series of dependencies for what were considered secondary services. Soon it was realised that there was a need for large, airy and light-flooded areas where the sick could be attended, so that what was originally referred to as the *Corredor del Sol* (sun corridor) was created. The first designs for this were by Juan Bautista de Toledo, who conceived it as a great belvedere, similar to the ones by Giulio Romano, joined to the *Torre de la Botica* (apothecary tower) by a long iron gallery. After the decision was made to increase the number of friars, this section became too small; consequently Juan de Herrera added a second, somewhat smaller perpendicular wing, thus creating the *Galería de Convalecientes* as we see it today.

The first floor is conceived as a delicate symmetrical interplay of the Serlian motif -an alternation of arched, linteled openings with different forms of spaces between the columns- on Doric columns on bases. This same rhythm is re-

*The Monks' Garden from
the Gallery of Convalescents.*

peated on the second floor, although here all the openings are
linteled and the columns are Ionic.

The complex was completed some years later when it was
decided to move all the health and sanitary services away
from the monastery, creating thus the *Casa de la Botica* (Apothecary House). This new building was constructed by Francisco de Mora, a pupil of Juan de Herrera who followed in the
stylistic footsteps of his master.

9.- OTHER DEPENDENCIES

As the work on the monastery neared completion, it was realised that the building was too small to contain all the functions for which it was destined. Its different areas -above all the public palace- were modified so that full advantage of all the constructed space could be taken. Even this was not enough, however, and it soon became clear that Juan de Herrera would have to design new buildings to house these services.

Thus it was that the first and second *Casa de Oficios*, aligned opposite the north façade, beyond *La Lonja*, the *Casa de la Botica*, the *Cachicanía*, and the *Pozo de la Nieve* came into being. The functions housed in these new dependencies were those considered "impure", following the layout established in the Temple of Jerusalem.

Also part of this programme was the construction of the recreational and work areas and buildings for the monks -the *Campillo* (vegetable patch), the *Castañar* (chestnut grove), the forge and the monastery- and the Church of San Bartolomé. This church, the work of Francisco de Mora, was set aside for the inhabitants of El Escorial, making it unnecessary for them to go to San Lorenzo.

In the XVIII century Juan de Villanueva, following this same plan, built the *Casa de Infantes*, the servants' quarters for the Infantes Don Gabriel, Don Antonio and Don Francisco Javier, the sons of Charles III. The work was carried out between 1770 and 1776 and with it the alignment was completed of the eastern façade of the monastery. In 1785 the same architect was commissioned to build the *Casa de Oficios del Ministerio de Estado*, today called the *Casa de Ministros*, thus completing the same project on the northern façade.

III.- THE "CASITAS" OR SMALL PALACES FOR RECREATION

Between 1771 and 1775, the Madrid architect Juan de Villanueva built for the Royal Site two small palaces for recreation, under the orders of Charles III, for his two eldest sons, the Prince of Asturias, Don Carlos, and the Infante Don Gabriel. This project for extending the royal residences with leisure pavilions is a European artistic phenomenon typical of the late XVIII century. While in France these constructions are referred to as *Trianons* or *Hermitages,* in Spain they were given the name of *Casitas* or *Casinos.*

The renovation of classical tastes, which sought grandiose and, to a certain extent, theatrical settings for rococo aesthetics, fostered the creation of this kind of palace. The *casitas* are genuine architectural caprices, in which forms are combined in the search for absolute perfection. These tiny marvels are surrounded by beautiful gardens, designed according to the strict laws of reason, which form an integral part of the artistic whole.

Each element was studied down to the last detail and thus, decoration became one of the greatest challenges to be faced by artists and architects alike. The quality and quantity of ornamental objects, as well as their variety and rarity, converted their owner into a "dilettante" of works of art. This is one of the most interesting aspects of tastes at the end of the XIX and beginning of the XX centuries, and led these maecenas to create *gabinetes* in the style of the renaissance "halls of wonders".

View of the Cachicanía and la Casa de la Nieve
from the Monks' Garden.

These constructions, together with those built in other Royal Sites, can be described globally as "court country houses" and were used by members of the royal family as places to escape from the strict rules of palace etiquette. The *casitas* were the centre of both lively literary and scientific debates and of music academies, where the royal hosts mingled with their guests and took an active part in these amusements which otherwise were often forbidden to them by protocol. In short, they were places of leisure and recreation where the nobility retired in search of the ideal of life: Enlightened Happiness, within a lifestyle ordered by reason, far from the grave social and political problems that were to be the detonating factor for the French Revolution.

The "Casita del Príncipe" or "Casita de Abajo"

The *Casita del Príncipe* is one of Juan de Villanueva's finest works and one of the most interesting examples of XVIII-century "total architecture". The pavilion was built in an oak forest on a hill between the monastery and the village of El Escorial, hence its alternative name ("Little House Below"). Our visit cannot be restricted to the different rooms and halls open to the public; it must also include a long and attentive walk through the gardens, which is where our itinerary begins.

Gardens

Having entered through the first gate and crossed the park, we come to the gardens. The visit commences (once we have passed the wrought iron grille with the monogram of Charles IV and María Luisa) in the landscaped area with the palace in the centre of the composition at the end of a straight line from the entrance. This almost imperceptible line divides both the building and the gardens into two symmetrical halves in counterpart to the transversal lines formed by the buildings. The entrance, with its two pavilions, serves to divide the park and the garden while the *casita*, with its two side wings, performs the same function as regards the front and rear gardens. The layout of the site is therefore governed entirely by these lines.

The front and rear gardens are linked by two porticoes with Tuscan columns, situated on either side of the main building. These atriums mark the passage between the *casita* and its side sections, and thus the scheme of intersection of lines is repeated. A further point of union between the two gardens is the palace itself, since it has façades on both sides.

The first flower bed, semicircular in design, has a pond in the middle from which eight radial paths begin, conferring upon it the appearance of a star.

*Gardens behind the
Casita del Príncipe.*

The rear garden has had to adapt to the slope of the site, and is divided into two independent zones on different levels joined by ramps at the ends. The first of these zones is quadrangular, not only in form but also in the layout of hedges. The structure of the second level is more complex since it constitutes a smaller, inverted echo of the ellipsoidal form of the garden. In the middle there is a small pond designed to catch rainwater. Thanks to the sloping terrain, a rustic waterfall emerges from it.

Casita del Príncipe,
main façade.

The Building

The T-shaped layout of this building is the prototype which Villanueva would use in the conception of more important works, such as the Prado Museum or the Astronomical Observatory. Access is through a freestanding portico supported by four Tuscan columns of great beauty. This same scheme is repeated at the rear, although in a more simplified form, since the structure is incorporated into the building following the *in antis* model so characteristic of classical Greek Antiquity. The reason for this simplification is the fact that the building was constructed in two stages. During the first, begun on October 28 1771 and completed on October 7 1775, a rectangular, two-storey structure was built with richly moulded volumes.

Some years later, on October 15 1781, extension work on the palace began with the addition of the two halls which give the building its "T" shape. These two rooms, though higher, harmonise perfectly with the rest of the building. Work was finally finished on December 5 1784.

Decoration

From the moment when the Princes of Asturias began to conceive the decoration of this building, one of the most important collections of late XVIII-century art began to be formed. The palace became one of the most exquisite of all the crown's possessions, causing Antonio Ponz, author of *Viaje de España* (Madrid, 1788) to exclaim: "A whole book would be needed to describe all there is in the form of fine arts, different types of marble, flooring, ceilings, porcelain, jewels and precious furniture, as well as the fine gardens and other parts of this wonderful house".

Little remains of this original sumptuosity, however, since much of it formed part of the fabulous booty that Joseph Bonaparte took with him from Spain. The *casita* was once again decorated with great magnificence during the reign of Ferdi-

Main Dining Room with sideboard table.

View of the Zaguán and the Dining Room.

nand VII, but during the regency of María Cristina, the most important works kept here went to the Prado Museum, at that time the Royal Museum, for fear that they might fall into the hands of the Carlists. Its present-day furnishing was carried out during the reign of Alphonso XIII, under whose patronage the ceilings were restored.

Our visit is restricted to the first floor, beginning with a large hall, today known as the *Zaguán,* which during the first phase of the building was the main hall. The ceiling was decorated by Vicente Gómez and constitutes one of the most integral examples of the so-called Pompeian decorative style, since the themes adopted were inspired by the frescoes found in this Roman city. On one of the walls hangs the interesting canvas attributed to Annibale Carraci, representing *St. John the Baptist.* Above the doors there are four floral paintings by Miguel Parra, and flanking the door into the dining room two flower garlands with religious subjects, by Benito Espinós, and two paintings from the Flemish school. The first of these *The Encounter between Abraham and Melquisedec,* by the Rubens school, and the second *The Sacrifice of Isaac,* attributed to Frans Franken "the Elder". Finally mention must be made of the wall beading, the original one for the room made by Camille Pernon, from Lyon, on the basis of designs by Dugourc.

We now proceed into the *Sala Encarnada* (Encarnadine Room), so called because of the original colour of its walls, where we see interesting canvases by Lucas Jordán, outstanding among which is *The Fall of Phaeton.* In the stretch between the windows hangs an *Allegory of Religion* by Andrea Vaccaro. Above the door leading into the queen's private room hangs López Enguidanos' famous *Still Life with Watermelon.* The decoration is completed with Vicente Gómez's astounding ceiling in the Etruscan style, which differs from the Pompeian style in that scenes are eliminated in favour of architectural elements so delicate in form that they seem to float as a pure geometrical abstraction.

The following room, the *Gabinete de la Reina* or queen's private room, is of small dimensions and is outstanding for the pure geometrical decoration of its ceiling, the work of Manuel

Pérez. On the walls we find two canvases by the Italian Panini, depicting the *Main Hall of the Basilica of St. Peter's* and *The Collection of Cardinal Silvio Valenti Gonzaga*. Finally we can admire Parra's View of the Palace of St. Pius V in Valencia.

Our visit continues into the *Sala del Barquillo* (Cone Room), whose ceiling was painted by Manuel Pérez, who found his inspiration in the *Wedding of Aldobrand* in the Vatican. On the walls are four canvases by Lucas Jordán with scenes from the life of the Virgin, and three by Andrea Vaccaro, representing allegories of *Hope, Charity,* and *Fortitude*. Above the two consoles are six interesting bronze sculptures on the basis of models by Juan de Bolonia.

The last room in this part of the building is the *Sala Amarilla* (Yellow Hall). The ceiling is by Manuel Pérez, following the same geometrical style we saw in the *Gabinete*. On the walls of this small room hangs the interesting series of thirty-three late XVII-century paintings on vellum depicting the Life of Christ, the work of the German artist Juan Guillermo Baür.

After the corridor we reach the main hall, known as the dining room, in the centre of which we see the admirable table-display cabinet which was formerly kept in the *Sala del Aparador* in order to exhibit the most important pieces of rock crystal crockery in Ferdinand VII's collection. The table consists of a large top in different types of marble and jasper, supported by fifteen wooden Corinthian columns. On the walls hang eleven paintings by Lucas Jordán, outstanding among which are the large canvases depicting *The Conversion of St. Paul* and *The Death of Julian the Apostate*. There is also a *Christ Wearing the Crown of Thorns* by Guido Reni.

The stuccoed ceiling with gold ornamentation is the work of Juan Bautista Ferroni. All the rooms built when the palace was extended have stuccoed ceilings.

We now proceed to the *Sala del Café*, which is in fact the exit hall into the rear gardens. This small room is oval in shape and is decorated with four niches containing Roman busts, from the collection of sculptures put together in the Palace of San Ildefonso by Queen Elisabeth Farnese. In the centre, on a small, one-footed table, stands an elegant alabaster templet inside which there is a bust of Ferdinand VII. The stuccoed ceiling is also the work of Ferroni.

The first room in the right-hand wing is the *Sala Azul* (Blue Hall) or *Sala de Tortillones*. The ceiling decoration is the work of Juan Mata Duque and depicts the feats of Hercules. On the walls hang four canvases by Corrado Giaquinto, originally sketches for the decoration of the dome of the chapel of the *Palacio Nuevo* in Madrid. They represent *St. Hermenegild, St Mary of the Head, St. Isidore* and *St. Leander*. Between the windows we see a painting of *St. Catherine,* assumed to be a copy by El Domenichino of an original by Reni. There are also two feminine heads attributed to Bagline. Our description of this room finishes with the four famous paintings which, according to the old inventories, were executed in paste. These curious works are by the German Nicolás Engelbert, and depict *Moses Rescued from the Waters, Susan and the Old Men, The Sacrifice of Isaac* and *Joseph Deciphers the Pharaoh's Dreams*.

Our visit comes to an end in the *Salón Japelli*, so called because the Italian Luigi Japelli decorated the ceiling in 1793. The decoration consists of courtly scenes framed by elegant imitation architectural forms. On the walls hang six works by the Neapolitan Corrado Giaquinto, part of the large collection of sketches for the decoration of the ceilings of the *Palacio Nuevo*. The themes are three allegories of *Commerce, Magnanimity* and *Abundance* and three mythological scenes, *The Goddess Ceres, Apollo and Daphne* and *Adonis Wounded by Love*.

Coffee Room.

The "Casita del Infante" or "Casita de Arriba"

This second palace was built by Juan de Villanueva for the "amusement" of Don Gabriel de Borbón, Charles III's favourite son. Work began early in May 1772 and was completed during the last week of June 1775. The site chosen was the La Herrería estate, beside the road to Robledo. This position, higher than that of the monastery, is the reason why the palace is today known as the *Casita de Arriba* (House Above).

Building and Gardens

The structure of the complex -building and gardens- is enclosed and centres on the palace, which appears as a single, isolated building.

The palace, a square structure in granite, has undergone practically no modifications with the exception of the second floor, which is now thoroughly covered by the roof. In the original plan it was an open terrace. Each side has a façade with an entablement with a curved-profile frieze, the main one being outstanding for its two Ionic columns. The four façades form a double axis which unfolds and orders the gardens, forming an orthogonal layout.

This arrangement is due to the fact that the palace was conceived as a concert hall. This justifies the great height of the central hall and its four, large rectangular windows which connect it to the second floor, where it is assumed the musicians sat. The audience could seat themselves comfortably on the ground floor or stroll in the garden during the intervals. The Infante Don Gabriel was a great music lover and had great teachers, among them the Hieronymite friar Antonio Soler. It has always been assumed that Father Soler composed his Six Quintets for harpsichord, organ and bowed instruments for the opening ceremony of the palace, with the Infante himself on harpsichord.

The residence was used once again during the reign of Fer-

Casita del Infante,
main façade.

Main Room.

Salón Pompeyano.

dinand VII, and more recently by His Majesty King Juan Carlos, who lived here while he studied at the School of Alphonso XII.

Decoration

None of the original decoration has survived, even the painting on the ceiling being a later work.

Having passed through the entrance hall, we come to the main hall, a large, square room used for music concerts. On the walls are four canvases by the Italian Fernando Brambilla which describe the Royal Site of Aranjuez, and four by Mariano Sánchez, with views of *The Port of Tarragona, The Cape of San Antonio, The Pexayres Tower* and *The Castle of San Antón*. In the middle of the room on an elegant one-footed table stands an impressive clock in the form of a templet with eight columns, housing a globe. The work, in gilt bronze, was made in France in the XIX century. The complex is crowned by the dome attributed to Vicente Gómez, which represents the allegories of the four seasons symbolised by feminine figures. All this is framed by elegant decorative borders. From the middle of the ceiling hangs a Spanish crystal chandelier from the XIX century.

We now proceed to the *Salón de la Caza* (Hunting Salon), used by His Majesty as an office, and so called because of the small hunting scenes on the ceiling, which were inspired by XVII- century Flemish paintings. On the walls hang a further two canvases by the Italian Brambilla showing views of the Royal Site of Aranjuez; *The Villa de Muros* by Mariano Sánchez; a portrait of *Henriette of England, Dauphine of France*, attributed to the van Dyck school; an elegant protrait of a gentleman from the XVIII-century Spanish school, which for many years was thought to be a portrait of the Infante Don Gabriel; and a XIX-century Italian school *Landscape*.

The next room, which Don Juan Carlos used as a dining room,is decorated with four paintings of vases, two of which are attributed to Daniel Seghers and the other two to Juan de

*View of the Casita from
the back gardens.*

la Corte. A further outstanding element is the XIX-century French semi-spherical lamp adorned with crystal chains.

The last room included in our visit is the *Salón Pompeyano*, so called because of its ceiling decoration; the paintings include an interesting version of Guido Reni's *St. Catherine*, attributed to El Domenichino; a *View of Almería* by Mariano Sánchez; and four XVIII-century porcelain plaques from El Buen Retiro, painted with pastoral scenes. Our visit concludes with a stroll through the gardens, from which it is possible to enjoy one of the finest views of the Monastery of San Lorenzo.

*View of the Monastery from
the Casita del Infante.*

BIOGRAPHY OF THE MOST
IMPORTANT ARTISTS

AGÜERO, Benito Manuel (1626-1670). Spanish painter, born and died in Madrid, pupil of Juan Bautista del Mazo. Famous for landscapes, battle scenes and views of fortifications.

ARCA, Niccolo delle (?-1494). Pupil of Jacopo della Quercia. Famous for having finished the tomb, begun by Niccolá Pisano, of Santo Domingo (roof of the sarcophagus),

ARFE Y VILLAFAÑE, Juan de (1535-1603). Spanish silversmith, engraver and sculptor. Commissioned by Philip II, he finished several statues destined for San Lorenzo. In 1597 he was ordered to make 64 bronze busts of saints worked in repousse for the Monastery.

ARIAS FERNÁNDEZ, Antonio (1620-1684). Pupil of Pedro de las Cuevas. A highly precocious painter, at 24 years of age he had already achieved considerable prestige, above all as a colourist.

BAROCCI, Federico, known as Fiori da Urbino (1535-1612). Pupil of Bautista Franco. Born in Urbino, he was author of the *Vocation of St. Andrew and St. Paul* for the Brotherhood of St. Andrew (Pésaro) and donated to Philip II by Duke Francesco.

BARROSO, Miguel (1538-1590). Spanish painter born in Consuegra (Toledo) and pupil of Becerra. In 1589 he was appointed court painter by Philip II.

BASSANO, Jacopo da Ponte (1515-1592). An Italian painter with major colourist ideas, his work covers a wide range of subjects, from the most peaceful country landscapes to the most complicated biblical scenes.

BAUR, Juan Guillermo (1600-1640). German miniaturist and engraver; pupil of Federico Brendel, although he completed his training in Italy.

BOSCH, Hieronymus van Aeken (c. 1450-1516). Flemish painter born in Hertogenbosch. Favourite painter of Philip II, who acquired his works through his secretary, Felipe de Guevara. Most of his genuine works are preserved in Spain.
BRAMBILLA, Fernando (1798-1832). Italian painter, born in Guerra. Author of a collection of views of all the Royal Sites. (The figures were painted by Manuel Miranda). Ferdinand VII appointed him court painter.

BREVOST, Giles and Michel: Flemish organ-makers of the XVI century. Philip II summoned them to San Lorenzo where, between 1579 and 1584, they built the organ for the Prior's Choir.

CAMBIAGO, Paolo: Italian sculptor who, together with Jacobo Trezzo the Younger, made the inlay for the mantle of the statue of Philip II in attitude of prayer.

CAMBIASSO, Luca, known as Luqueto (1527-1585). Italian painter, born in Moneglia (Genoa). He arrived in San Lorenzo in 1583 to work on the choir vault. His dry, mannerist style greatly disappointed the King.

CAMBIASSO, Orazio (XVI-century). Son of Luca Cambiasso, with whom he came to Spain in 1583. He collaborated in, amongst other works, the decoration of the *Sala de Batallas* and Chapter Rooms.

CANO, Alonso (1601-1667). Spanish sculptor, architect and painter born in Granada. Pupil of the sculptor Juan Martínez Montañés and the painter Francisco Pacheco, he worked with the painter Juan del Castillo and, according to some, Herrera the Elder. He was a protégé of Velázquez.

CARBONELLE, Alonso (?-1660). Spanish sculptor and architect who worked with Eugenio Caxés. He carried out the project for the entrance door, staircase, altar and flooring of the Royal Pantheon.

CARDUCHO, Bartolomé (1560-1608). Italian painter, sculptor and architect, born in Florence. Pupil of Bartolomé Ammanati (Florence) and of Federico Zúccaro, with whom he travelled to Spain as an assistant when the latter was contracted by the Count-Duke of Olivares, Philip II's Ambassador. In San Lorenzo he worked under the orders of Tibaldi.

CARDUCHO, Vicente (1576-1638). Spanish painter born in Florence. At a very early age he came to Spain with his brother Bartolomé. On the death of his brother, Philip III appointed him Court Painter.

CARREÑO DE MIRANDA, Juan (1614-1685). Spanish painter born in Avilés (Asturias). Pupil of Juan de las Cuevas and Bartolomé Román. Philip IV appointed him court painter in 1669 and Charles II appointed him assistant to the head palace steward in 1671.

CARVAJAL, Luis de (1534-1607). Spanish painter born in Toledo, brother of the sculptor Juan Bautista Monegro and pupil of Juan de Villoldo. Philip II appointed him court painter.

CASTELLO, Fabrizio (1554-1617). Spanish painter who arrived from Italy with his father Giambattista Castello in 1577. He trained with his brother Nicolás Granello and Francisco de Urbino. In 1611, he was commissioned by Philip III to paint 48 of the reliquary-busts which had been sculpted by Juan de Arfe.

CASTELLO, Giambattista, Il Bergamasco (1509-1569). Italian painter and architect born in Bergamo. According to Father Sigüenza, he drew the first plans for the principal staircase.

CELLINI, Benvenuto (1500-1571). Italian stone cutter, jeweller, sculptor, medallion maker and writer born in Florence. According to Michaelangelo "he was an incomparable artist in the finishing of forms and richness of painstaking details."

CENSORE, Clemente. A XVII-century bronze worker from Milan who worked with Fenelli on the lamp for the Royal Pantheon.

CERVANTES, Nicolás. XIX-century silversmith from Madrid. Together with the silversmith Manuel García he made the lamp for the presbytery of the basilica.

CINCINATO, Rómulo (1502-1600). Painter born in Florence, pupil of Francesco Salviati. By appointment to Philip II, he was contracted together with Patricio Caxés, by Luis de Requesens.

COMANE, Giovanni Battista. XVI-century sculptor. Associated with Pompeo Leoni and Jacopo da Trezzo. He was appointed to be in charge of the architectural work of the project by Herrera for the main altar of the Basilica.

COXCIE, Michel, known as the Flemish Raphael (1499-1592). Flemish painter born in Malinas, pupil of Bernard van Orley. Even though his originals earned him considerable prestige, his work as a copyist for Philip II was also highly esteemed.

CRESCENZI, Giovanni Battista (1595-1660). Italian architect and painter born in Rome. Recommended to Philip III by Cardinal Zapata to work on the Royal Pantheon. Thanks to the favour of the Count-Duke of Olivares he became a knight of the military order of Saint James.

DAVID, Gerard (c. 1460-1523). Flemish painter born in Oudewater. He was considered to be the first Flemish painter to introduce Italian renaissance elements into the Nordic traditions.

ESPINÓS, Benito (1748-1818). Spanish painter born in Valencia. He was a professor of floral and adornment painting in the School of Fine Arts of San Carlos, in Valencia.

FENELLI, Virgilio. Italian artist, author of the lamp for the Royal Pantheon.

FERRONI, Giovanni Battista. Italian artist, author of the stucco work in the *Casita del Príncipe* in San Lorenzo and El Pardo.

FLECHA, Guiseppe. Italian cabinet-maker, author of the choir seats in the Old Church and Morals Classroom, carried out according to the design by Herrera.

FONTANA, Lavinia (1552-1602). Italian painter born in Rome. Daughter of the painter Próspero Fontana, and wife and collaborator of the painter Pablo Zappi.

FRÍAS ESCALANTE, Juan Antonio de (1633-1669). Spanish painter born in Córdoba and active in Madrid. Precocious artist, pupil of Rizzi. Admirer of Venetian painting and interested in the work of Cano and Herrera Barnuevo.

GÁLVEZ, Juan (1774-1847). Spanish painter born in Mora (Toledo). He studied in the Academy of Fine Arts of San Fernando, where he was director and teacher of drawing.

GARCÍA, Manuel (?-1838). Spanish painter who, together with silversmith Cervantes, made the lamp for the presbytery in the Basilia of San Lorenzo.

GENTILESCHI, Artemisia (1593- c. 1652). Italian painter born in Rome. Daughter and pupil of Horacio Gentileschi, she travelled with him to England, where she painted numerous portraits.

GHEIN, Peter van der. Flemish carillon maker from the XVI century who made the first carillon, "organ of bells", for the monastery.

GIAQUINTO, Corrado (1700-1765). Italian painter born in Mofelta. He was summoned to Spain by Philip V to make several ceilings in the *Palacio Nuevo* in Madrid.

GIORDANO, Lucca, known in Spain as Lucas Jordán (1632-1705). Pupil of Ribera and Pedro de Cortona. Italian painter born in Naples. In 1692 he was summoned by Charles II to decorate the ceilings of the Basilica of San Lornezo.

GÓMEZ, Pedro. Penman active towards the end of the XVI century, born in Cuenca. In 1581 he was summoned to San Lorenzo to work on the composition of the choir books.

GÓMEZ DE LA FUENTE, Domingo. Spanish sculptor active towards the end of the XVI century, he worked on the Infantes' Pantheon.

GÓMEZ DE MORA, Juan (1586- c. 1646). Spanish architect born in Madrid. Nephew and pupil of Fernando de Mora. He was master builder for the Royal Palaces in Madrid and El Pardo.

GÓMEZ NOVELLA, Vicente. Spanish painter born in Valencia, active towards the end of the XVIII century.

GÓMEZ DE VILLASEÑOR, Juan (?-1597). He was court painter of Philip II, and as such carried out different works in San Lorenzo and retouched others.

GONZÁLEZ, Bartolomé (1564-1627). Spanish painter born in Valladolid. Pupil of Patricio Caxés and, as from 1617, was court painter of Philip III.

GOTEN, Jacobo van der (1706-1768). French weaver summoned by Philip V to found the Royal Tapestry Factory of Santa Bárbara.

GRANELLO, Nicolás (?-1593). Italian painter born in Genoa. Son and pupil of El Bergamasco, with whom he worked on the paintings in the new tower of the Alcázar in Madrid. He was commissioned by Philip II to go to San Lorenzo together with the other Genoese painters.

GRECO, El. Domenikos Theotokopoulos (1541-1614). Painter born in Candía (Crete). In 1576, he arrived in Spain from Rome in search of work. Whilst waiting to be summoned to San Lorenzo by Philip II he settled in Toledo where he later took up residence after the failure of his *St. Mauritius*.

GUERCINO, Giovan Francesco (1591-1666). Italian painter born in Cento. His work combines the grandiosity of the school of Bologna, with the colours of Caravaggio.

GUIDI, Domenico (1625-1701). Italian sculptor born in Torano. Pupil of Algardi in Rome.

GUTIÉRREZ DE TORICES, Father Eugenio (?-1709). Spanish sculptor and Mercedarian friar born in Madrid. In his leisure time he worked on flowers and fruit with wax crayons and colours and was admired by the artists of his era.

HAMEN Y LEÓN, Juan van der (1596-1631). Spanish painter born in Madrid. Outstanding for his still-lifes.

HAZE, Melchor de. Flemish carillon maker who towards the end of the XVII century made the second carillon for the monastery.

HERRERA, Juan de (1530-1597). Spanish architect born in Mobellán (Cantabria). Following the death of Juan Bautista de Toledo he took charge of the construction of San Lorenzo which, thanks to his impressive organizing capabilities, he managed to finish in record time.

HERRERA BARNUEVO, Sebastián (1619-1671). Spanish painter, sculptor and architect born in Madrid. He studied under his father, and later with Alonso Cano. Amongst other things he was curator of the Royal Site of San Lorenzo and chief master builder for the Villa Madrid and Buen Retiro.

HOLANDA, Rodrigo. Spanish painter from the end of the XVI century, to whom are attributed the copies of the mural paintings allusive to the French Campaign in the *Sala de Batallas*.

JAPELLI, Luigi. Italian painter from the end of the XVIII century. He worked on the wall decoration in the *Casita del Principe*.

LANDECH. Spanish architect from the beginning of the XX century. He designed the tomb of María Teresa de Borbón, sister of Alphonso XIII.

LANFRANCO, Giovanni (1581-1647). Italian painter born in Parma. He was a pupil of Agostino Carracci.

LEHR, André. Dutch carillon maker, he built the carillon at present in the Monastery of San Lorenzo.

LEONARDO, Juseppe (1601-1656). Spanish painter born in Calatayud. Pupil of Eugenio de Caxés. He settled in Madrid where he died a madman.

LEONI, León (1509-1590). Italian architect, sculptor and medallion maker born in Menaggio (Como). He worked in the service of the Emperor Charles V.

LEONI, Pompeius (1553-1608). Italian sculptor born in Pavia. He was summoned by Philip II to carry out the majority of the sculptures in bronze for San Lorenzo.

LEYNIER, Daniel and Daniel. Flemish tapestry-makers from the beginning of the XVIII century who wove the Telemachus series for Philip V.

LIBORNA Echeverría, Pedro. Spanish organ-maker from the end of the XVII century. He reconstructed the organs of the basilica after the fire in 1671.

LIZARGÁRATE, Pedro de (1629-?). Spanish architect born in Toledo. He worked in the Royal Pantheon, responsible for the arrangement and execution of the stone works.

LÓPEZ ENGUÍDANOS, José (1760-1812). Spanish painter and engraver born in Valencia. He was the king's court painter.

MADRID, Brother Nicolás de. Hieronymite friar of the XVII century, responsible for the drainage and ventilation system of the Royal Pantheon.

MAELLA, Mariano Salvador de (1739-1819). Spanish painter born in Valencia. After his training in Valencia and his sojourn in Rome, in 1765 entered into the service of the King, under the orders of Mengs. He became court painter.

MAESO, Angel. Spanish cabinet-maker from the beginning of the XIX century. He finished the so-called "fine wood" suite of rooms.

MARATTA, Carlo (1625-1713). Italian painter born in Camurano. Pupil of Andrea Sacchi and protégé of Pope Alexander VII. Specialist in religious themes.

MARZAL, José. XIX-century Spanish artist, author of the plaster frames for the paintings of the basilica.

MATA Duque, Juan. Spanish painter from the end of the XVIII century. He decorated several of the ceilings of the *Casita del Príncipe*.

MELÉNDEZ, Luis (1716-1780). Spanish painter born in Naples. Pupil of his father, Francisco Meléndez. After his return from Rome, he worked on the illumination for the choir books in the palace chapel. He specialized in still-lifes.

METSYS, Quintín (1465/6-1580). Flemish painter born in Louvain. In 1491 he obtained the title of Maestro in Antwerp and became one of the foremost artists in the city.

MONEGRO, Juan Bautista (1545-1621). Spanish sculptor and architect born in Toledo. Philip II summoned him to San Lorenzo to produce the most important stone sculptures.

MONTALVO, Bartolomé (1769-1846). Spanish painter born in Sangarcía (Segovia). Pupil of Zacarías Velázquez, he was director of the Academy of Fine Arts of San Fernando from 1819 until his death.

MONTIEL, José. Spanish painter of the XVII century. Few of his works are known.

MORA, Francisco de (1553-1610). Spanish architect born in Cuenca. Pupil and assistant of Juan de Herrera, who recommended him to Philip II as the most excellent teacher to have ever served under him.

MORETTO DA BRESCIA, Alessandro Bonvicino (1498-1555). Italian painter born in Povato. A discreet and excellent colourist. He became known as a painter of religious compositions for which he prepared himself through fasting and prayer.

MORO, Antonio (1519-1576). Flemish painter born in Utrecht. Protégé of Cardinal Granvella, who recommended him to Philip II, who ordered him to paint numerous portraits. On two occasions he travelled to Spain.

NANI, Mariano (1725-1804). Italian painter born in Naples. He came to the court of Charles III to paint models of tapestries, rugs and ornamental cloths.

NAVARRETE, Juan Fernández, known as El Mudo ("the Mute") (1526-1579). Spanish painter born in Logroño. After training in Spain he travelled to Italy where he worked with Titian and Tibaldi. In 1566 he worked in San Lorenzo. In 1568 Philip II appointed him Painter to the King. Almost all of his known works are preserved in the monastery and, despite his constant illnesses, he was extraordinarily prolific.

NOVELLI, Pietro il Monrealese (1603-1647). Italian painter born in Monreale. He is considered one of the best Sicilian painters.

NUZZI, Mario, known as "dei Fiori" (1603-1673). Italian painter born in Penna (Fermo). He specialized in floral works, for which reason he was nicknamed "Fiori".

OERTEL, Abraham, known as "Ortelius" (1527-1598). Flemish geographer born in Antwerp. An important map engraver who, in 1575, thanks to the help of Arias Montano, was appointed geographer to Philip II. He was nicknamed the Ptolemy of the XVI century.

OLMO, José de. Spanish architect from the end of the XVII century, he worked on the Altar of the Sacred Form in San Lorenzo.

PACIOTTO, Francesco (1521-1591). Italian military engineer known in Spain as "Pachote". His opinions on the project of Juan Bautista de Toledo were noted by Philip II, who demanded new plans for the Temple be drawn up.

PALMA, Jacopo, "Il Giovane" (1544-1628). Italian painter born in Venice. His style of painting was somewhat repetitive, although he was noted for his paintings of heads.

PANTOJA DE LA CRUZ, Juan (1553-1608). Spanish painter born in Valladolid. Pupil and collaborator of Sánchez Coello with whom he shared the honor of court painter and the esteem of Philip II. He gained considerable prestige in portrait painting.

PARRA, Miguel (1784-1846). Spanish painter born in Valencia. He studied with Espinós and Vicente López. He was court painter of Ferdinand VII and Isabella II.

PATINIR, Joaquín (c.1485-1524). Flemish painter who is considered initiator of landscape painting as an independent genre.

PERNON, Camille. French weaver, active towards the end of the XVIII century. He carried out numerous works for the Spanish court.

PERRET, Pedro (1555-1637). Flemish engraver born in Antwerp. In 1587, whilst serving Philip II, he engraved in copper the drawings by Herrera of the Monastery of San Lorenzo.

POLO, Diego (1610-1655). Spanish painter born in Burgos. Nephew of Diego Polo "the Elder". He studied with Antonio Lanchares. He gained considerable prestige with his colour work classed as "hot".

PONZ, Antonio (1725-1792). Spanish painter and writer, born in Bechí (Castellón). Author of *Viaje de España* (1772-1794), 18 vols., the work which constituted the first attempt to catologue Spanish monuments.

PONZANO GASCÓN, Ponciano (1813-1877). Spanish sculptor born in Zaragoza. His Majesty's Court sculptor and teacher of drawing and modelling in the Academy of San Fernando.

RENI, Guido (1575-1642). Italian painter born in Calvenzano. He divided his time between Bologna and Rome where he became influenced by Caravaggio before eventually returning to the balanced style of Raphaelesque tradition of the Bologna school.

REYMERSWAELE, Marinus (?-1567). Flemish painter born in Zeeland. One of the most important cultivators of genre painting of the XVI century.

RIBERA, José de (1591-1652). Spanish painter born in Játiva (Valencia). Even though all his works were carried out in Naples, he never forgot his Spanish origin and thus became known by the nickname of "El Españoleto". Together with Velázquez he is the Spanish painter of most international fame.

RIZZI, Francisco (1614-1685). Spanish painter born in Madrid. Pupil of Vicente Carducho. In 1656 he was appointed painter to the King.

ROLDÁN, Luisa (1656-1704). Spanish sculptress born in Seville. Daughter and pupil of Pedro Roldán. She became famous for small clay sculptures.

SÁNCHEZ, Mariano (1740-1822). Spanish painter born in Valencia. He studied in the Academy of Fine Arts of San Fernando (Madrid). He won several prizes and, on the basis of his merits, earned the position of supernumerary academic. Charles III commissioned him to paint all the Spanish ports (120 canvases) and was so pleased that he appointed him court painter.

SÁNCHEZ COELLO, Alonso (1531/32-1588). Spanish painter born in Benifairó (Valencia.). He worked in Portugal in the service of Prince Joao, brother-in-law to Philip II and, on his death, went to work for the Spanish King, who held him in great esteem.

SEGHERS, Daniel (c.1592-1661). Flemish painter born in Antwerp. He was a pupil of Jan Brueghel, who converted him to Catholicism. Later he became a Jesut. He is known as "painter of flowers and the flower of all painters."

SERRANO. Spanish cabinet maker of the XVI century who, under the orders of Flecha, worked with Gamboa in the carpentry of the Choir, Old Church and Morals Classroom.

SON, Joris van (1623-1667). Flemish painter, baptized in Antwerp. He devoted himself to still lifes. In 1644 he was master in Antwerp.

TACCA, Pietro (1580-1640). Italian sculptor born in Carrara. Pupil of Juan de Bologna whom he assisted in several works.

TAVARONE, Lázaro (1556-1641). Italian painter born in Genoa. Pupil of Cambiasso, with whom he came to Spain to assist in the work in San Lorenzo.

TIBALDI, Pellegrino Pellegrini il (1527-1596). Italian painter and architect born in Perugia. He studied painting and architecture in Bologna, and in Rome with Volterra. In 1564 he became protégé of Cardinal Carlos Borromeo, thanks to whom he was able to follow a successful and fecund career as architect, engineer and adviser. By virtue of his considerable reputation, Philip II summoned him to San Lorenzo.

TINTORETTO, Doménico (1556-1635). Italian painter born in Venice. Pupil of his father, Jacopo. He gained prestige as a portrait painter of the most important personages of his era.

TINTORETTO, Jacopo Robusti il (1518-1594). Italian painter born in Venice. Maximum representative of mannerist painting from the end of the Renaissance period in Venice.

TISI, Benvenuto Garofalo, (1481-1559). Italian painter born in Ferrara. His brilliant compositions are gentle, natural, and gracious, and some-what archaic in style. His strong colours are full of sentiment.

TIZIANO VECELLIO (Titian) (1485-1576). Italian painter born in Peive di Cadore (Tyrol). He is considered the best painter of the Venetian school and one of the most important figures in the history of art. His contact with Austria House began when he painted the portrait of Charles V at the beginning of 1530. In 1533, as reward for his work and friendship with the Emperor he received the title of Count Palatino and Knight of the Gold Spur. His relationship with Philip II was much closer, and fruit of this are the paintings preserved in the Prado Museum and in San Lorenzo.

TOLEDO, Juan Bautista de (?-1567). Spanish architect, born in Madrid. By virtue of his Italian training under Michaelangelo, in the Vatican Basilica, in 1559 he was summoned by Philip II to act as director of all the royal works. His most important work is the universal plan of the Monastery of San Lorenzo.

TOMKINSON, Thomas. English piano maker from the beginning of the XIX century.

TREZZO, Jacoppo da (1515-1589). Italian sculptor born in Milan and better known as "Jacometrezzo". He worked with Pompeius Leoni and Juan Bautista Comane on the main altarpiece of the basilica, specializing in the extraction, cutting and fitting of the stones and the casting and gilding of the metal used.

TREZZO, Jacobo known as "El Mozo" (?-1601). Italian sculptor, nephew of "Jacometrezzo", who went to Spain to help his uncle.

URBINA, Diego (?-1593). Spanish painter born in Madrid. He was court painter to Philip II. His drawing was precise and he obtained an exquisite colouring, nevertheless his figures were somewhat mannerist.

URBINO, Francisco de (?-1582). Italian painter born in Genoa. He came to Spain together with Bergamasco to assist in the works of the Alcázar. On the death of Bergamasco, Philip II put him in charge of finishing the work, which he did with the help of his brothers Juan Mata and Juan María

VACCARO, Andrea (1598-1670). Italian painter born in Naples. Pupil of Caravaggio and Dominiquino, he obtained distinction thanks to the brilliance of his technique.

VEGA, Gaspar (?-1576). Spanish architect, probably born in Seville. He worked in San Lorenzo as advisor to Philip II, carrying out appraisals and drawing up reports and plans.

VELÁZQUEZ, Diego (1599-1660). Spanish painter born in Seville. Thanks to his being appointed head palace steward he was able to work in San Lorenzo on the collection of paintings for the sacristy and chapter rooms.

VERONESE, Carletto (1570-?). Italian painter born in Venice. Son and pupil of Paolo Veronese.

VERONESE, Paolo Caliari (1525-1588). Italian painter born in Verona. His works are distinguished for their sumptuousness and beauty, his painting being the best reflection of luxury and refinement of Venetian society towards the end of the XVI century.

VILLACASTÍN, Father Antonio de (1512-1603). Spanish Hieronymite friar born in Villacastín (Toledo). He worked in San Lorenzo as chief master builder, finally acquiring such an outstanding role that from 1670 all the works carried out needed his written approval.

VILLANUEVA, Juan de (1731-1811). Spanish architect born in Madrid. He studied in the Academy of Fine Arts of San Fernando, winning several prizes which helped him to be appointed draughtsman, under the orders of his brother, Diego, in the works of the Royal Palace. He received a grant to study in Rome, from whence he returned in 1756. His first work for Charles III was the construction of the *Casa de Infantes* in San Lorenzo.

VOS. Martín (1532-1603). Flemish painter born in Antwerp. After his formative period he travelled to Italy where he collaborated with Tintoretto. He took up residence in Antwerp, and became deacon of the bro-therhood of painters of this city.

VRIENDT, Frans, known as Floris (1529-1570). Flemish painter born in Antwerp. He is noted for the enormous care, study and perfection of his work, which however lacks sentiment.

VRIES, Adriaen de (1560-1603). Flemish sculptor and painter born in The Hague. He worked in Milan in the studio of Pompeius Leoni, collaborating in the sculptures for the presbytery of the basilica.

WEDLINGEN, Juan de. Hungarian mathematician born in Prague. He was the author of the solar adjusters in the Palace of the House of Austria.

WEYDEN, Roger van der (c.1400-1464). Flemish painter born in Tournai. His work is noted for its perfect beauty, superb execution and deep, profound sentiment, where the sweet, pathetic and tender meets with the vigorous.

ZÚCCARO, Federico (1542-1609). Italian painter born in San Angelo in Vado (Urbino). An artist of great prestige, he was invited by Philip II to work in San Lorenzo. His work did not please the Monarch who, after the artist had left Spain in 1588, demanded that it all be retouched except for the painting on the main altar.

ZUMBIGO, Bartolomé. Spanish artist from the middle of the XVII century, author of the porphyry lights of the library.

ZURBARÁN, Francisco (1598-1664). Spanish painter born in Fuente de Cantos (Badajoz). His style combines severity and reality with spiritual intensity, making him the painter who best responded to the stringent aesthetic ideals of the Spanish religious orders.

BIBLIOGRAPHY AND EXHIBITIONS.

A.- Bibliography

AGUILÓ, M. P.: "La ebanistería alemana en el Monasterio de El Escorial", in *Real Monasterio-Palacio de El Escorial*. Unpublished studies from the IV Centenary of the termination of the works. Madrid, 1987.

AMEZÚA, R. G. de: "Los nuevos órganos del Real Monasterio de El Escorial", in *Reales Sitios*, no. 3., 1965, pp. 62-69.

AZNAR, F.: *El Monasterio de San Lorenzo el Real de El Escorial*. Madrid, 1985.

ALVAREZ TURIENZO, T.: *El Escorial en las letras españoles*. Madrid, 1985.

BENITO DOMÉNECH, F.; "La pintura religiosa en Alonso Sánchez Coello", in *Alonso Sánchez Coello y el retrato en la Corte de Felipe II*. Madrid, 1990.

BERMEJO, D.; *Descripción del Real Monasterio de San Lorenzo del Escorial*. Madrid, 1820.

BRAUNFELS, W.: *La Arquitectura Monacal en Occidente*. Barcelona, 1975.

BROWN, J.: "Las pinturas de Zurbarán en la sacristía de Guadalupe", in *Imágenes e ideas en la pintura española del siglo XVII*. Madrid, 1985, pp. 143-177.
"Felipe IV, el rey de coleccionistas" in *Fragmentos*, no. 11., 1987, pp. 4-20.
"Obras maestras en la colección de pintura del Patrimonio Nacional", in *Reales Sitios*, special issue, 1989, pp. 68-74.
La Edad de Oro de la pintura en España. Madrid, 1990.

BUSTAMANTE GARCÍA, A.: "El Escorial: una leyenda viva", in *Reales Sitios*, special issue, 1989, pp. 75-86.

CORRECHER, C. M.: "Jardines del Real Monasterio de San Lorenzo de El Escorial". *Reales Sitios*, no. 78 (1983) & 80 (1984).

ESTELLA, Margarita: "Introducción a la escultura del siglo XVII en Madrid", in *El Arte en la época de Calderón*. Madrid, 1981.

GARCIA-FRIAS Checa, C.: *La Pintura mural y de caballete en la Biblioteca del Real Monasterio de El Escorial*. Madrid, 1991.

GUERRA DE LA VEGA, R.: *Juan de Villanueva, Arquitecto del Principe de Asturias (Carlos IV)*. Madrid, 1986.

HERNÁNDEZ, L.: "La liturgia solemne de los Jerónimos en el Monasterio de El Escorial". *Reales Sitios*, no. 80, Madrid, 1984, pp. 65-72.

HERNÁNDEZ FERRERO, J.: "Cuarenta y cinco empresas filipenses" in *IV Centenario del Monasterio de El Escorial. Fe y Sabiduría. La Biblioteca*. Madrid, 1986, pp. 15-20.
"Consideraciones sobre los origenes históricos del Monasterio de El Escorial", in *Real Monasterio-Palacio de El Escorial*. Unpublished studies from the IV Centenary of the termination of the works. Madrid, 1987, pp. 13-26.

HERRERO CARRETERO, C.: "Tapices donados para el culto de la iglesia vieja". *IV Centenario del Monasteio de El Escorial. Iglesia y Monarquia*. La Liturgia. Madrid, 1986, pp. 93-99.

HIGHFIELD, J. R.: "The Jeronimites in Spain, their Patrons and Success, 1373-1516", in *Journal of Ecclesiastical History*, vol. 34, no. 4., October, 1983, pp. 513-533.

JUNQUERA, J. J.: *La decoración y el mobiliario de los palacios de Carlos IV*. Madrid, 1979.

JUNQUERA DE VEGA, P. Herrero Carretero, C.: *Catálogo de Tapices del Patrimonio Nacional*. Vol. I: Siglo XVI. Madrid, 1986.

JUSTEL, B.: *La Real Biblioteca de El Escorial y sus manuscritos árabes*. Madrid, 1987.

KINDER, H. Hilgemann, W.: *Atlas histórico mundial*. Madrid, 1980.

KUBLER, G.: *La obra del Escorial*. Madrid, 1985.

LÓPEZ GAJATE, J.: "Escultura escurialense fundacional: el Cristo de Cellini", in *Real Monasterio de El Escorial*. Studies from the IV Centenary of the termination of the Monastery of San Lorenzo el Real de El Escorial. San Lorenzo de El Escorial, 1984, pp. 465-502.

LÓPEZ SERRANO, M.: *El Escorial*. Madrid, 1987.

LÓPEZ SERRANO, M. & Martín, F. A.: *Palacio Real de El Pardo*. Madrid, 1985.

LUNA, J. J.: "Jean Nocret y los retratos de la Corte de Luis XIV en Madrid", in *Cinco siglos de Arte en Madrid (siglos XV-XX)*. Madrid, 1991.

LLOP I BAYO, F.: "El Carillón del Real Monasterio de San Lorenzo de El Escorial. La restauración y recuperación de un patrimonio sonoro peculiar", in *Carillón del Real Monasterio de San Lorenzo de El Escorial. Recuperación de un patrimonio sonoro*. Madrid, 1988, pp. 13-28.

MARINI, R.: *La obra pictórica completa de Veronés*. Barcelona, 1976.

MARTÍN GÓMEZ, P.: *La Casa perpetua del Rey de España o las tumbas reales de El Escorial*. Madrid, 1987.

MARTÍN GONZÁLEZ, J. J.: "Estructura y tipología del retablo mayor del Monasterio de El Escorial", in *Real Monasterio-Palacio de El Escorial*. Unpublished studies from the IV Centenary of the termination of the works. Madrid, 1987, pp. 203-220.

MARTÍNEZ CUESTA, J.: "Las Salas Capitulares del Monasterio de San Lorenzo: actual ordenación de sus colecciones pictóricas", in *Real Sitios*, no. 103, 1990, pp. 37-44.
"La Antesala de Embajadores del Palacio de los Borbones", in *La Herrería*, no. 6, 1990, pp. 32-37.

MELENDRERAS GIMENO, J. L.: "El Panteón de Infantes de San Lorenzo de El Escorial", in *Real Sitios*, no. 88, 1986, pp. 37-44.

MODINO DE LUCAS, M.: *Los priores de la construccion del Monasterio de El Escorial*. Documentos para la Historia Escurialense (IX). Madrid, 1985.

MOLEÓN GAVILANES, P.: *La Arquitectura de Juan de Villanueva. El Proceso del Proyecto*. Madrid, 1988.
"El otro centro del laberinto. Consideraciones sobre el sotocoro del Monasterio de El Escorial", in *El Escorial. La Arquitectura del Monasterio*. Madrid, 1986, pp. 217-220.

MORÁN TURINA, J. M. & Checa Cremades, F.: *Las Casas del Rey. Casas de Campo, Cazaderos y Jardines. Siglos XVI y XVII*. Madrid, 1986.

NAVASCUÉS PALACIO, P.: "El Patio y Templete de los Evangelistas de El Escorial" in *Real Monasterio-Palacio de El Escorial*. Unpublished studies from the IV Centenary of the termination of the works. Madrid, 1987, pp. 61-74.

OSTEN SACKEN, C. von der: *El Escorial*. Iconological study. Madrid, 1984.

PÉREZ SÁNCHEZ, A. E. & Díez García, J. L.: *Catálogo de las Pinturas*. Museo Municipal de Madrid. Madrid, 1990.

POLERÓ, V.: *Catalogo de los cuadros del Real Monasterio de San Lorenzo, llamado de El Escorial*. Madrid, 1857.

PONZ, A: *Viaje de España*. Vol. II. Madrid, 1788.

PORTELA SANDOVAL, F. J.: "La escultura en el Monasterio de El Escorial" in *Fragmentos*, nos. 4-5. Madrid, 1985, pp. 96-113.

QUEVEDO, J.: *Historia del Real Monasterio de San Lorenzo*. Madrid, 1854.

RINCÓN GARCÍA, W.: "El programa iconográfico de las "parejas de santos" en la Basílica de San Lorenzo de El Escorial" in *Real Monasterio-Palacio de El Escorial*. Unpublished studies from the IV Centenary of the termination of the works. Madrid, 1987.

ROTONDO, A.: *Descripción de la Gran Basilica del Escorial*. Madrid, 1861.

RUBIO, L.: "Cronología y topografía de la fundación y construcción del Monasterio de San Lorenzo el Real", in *Monasterio de San Lorenzo el Real de El Escorial en el Cuarto Centenario de su Fundación*. Biblioteca "La Ciudad de Dios". Real Monasterio de El Escorial, 1964, pp. 11-70.

RUBIO, A.: *Antonio Soler. Catálogo Crítico*. Cuenca, 1980.

RUIZ ALCÓN, M. T.: "*Monasterio Real de El Escorial*. Madrid, 1987.
"Vida de Cristo: Cuadros de Juan Giullermo Baur. Monasterio de El Escorial", in *Reales Sitios*. no. 51, 1977, pp. 17-24.

SÁNCHEZ HERNÁNDEZ, L.: *Casas Reales del Patrimonio Nacional*. Madrid, 1988.

SANTOS OTERO, A. de: *Los evangelios apócrifos*. Critical bilingual edition. Madrid, 1979.

SCHUBERT, O.: *El Barroco en España*. Madrid, 1924.

SIGÜENZA, Fr. J.: *Fundación del Monasterio de El Escorial*. Madrid, 1963.

SULLIVAN, E. J.: *Baroque Painting in Madrid. The Contribution of Claudio Coello, with a Catologue Raisonné of His works*. Columbia, Mo., 1986.

TOVAR MARTÍN, V.: "El arquitecto Juan Gómez de Mora y su relación con lo "escurialense", in *Real Monasterio-Palacio de El Escorial*. Unpublished studies from the IV Centenary of the termination of the works. Madrid, 1987, pp. 185-202.

VALCANOVER, F.: *La obra pictórica completa de Tiziano*. Barcelona, 1974.

VICENTE Y GARCÍA, A.: *La escultura de Juan Bautista Monegro en el Real Monasterio de San Lorenzo de El Escorial*. Madrid, 1990.

XIMÉNEZ, A.: *Descripción del Real Monasterio de San Lorenzo del Escorial*. Madrid, 1764.

B.- Exhibitions.

Madrid/1985. El Escorial in the National Library. IV Centenary of the Monastery of El Escorial. National Library.

Madrid/1986. El Escorial. Biography of an Era. IV Centenary of the Monastery of El Escorial. National Library.

Madrid/1986. Centenary of the Monastery of El Escorial. Church and monarchy. La Liturgia. National Heritage.

Madrid/1986. IV Centenary of the Monastery of El Escorial. The Royal Houses. The Palace. National Heritage.

Madrid/1986. IV Centenary of the Monastery of El Escorial. The King's Collections. Paintings & Sculptures. National Heritage.

Madrid/1986. IV Centenary of the Monastery of El Escorial. Faith and Knowledge. The Library. National Heritage.

Madrid/1986. Factory and Construction (the Construction).
IV Centenary of the Monastery of El Escorial. The Autonomous Community of Madrid.

Madrid/1986. City and Monastery (the Environment). IV Centenary of the Monastery of El Escorial. The Autonomous Community of Madrid.